Chinese Phrase Book

*Over 1000 Essential Mandarin Phrases
You Don't Want to Be Without on Your
Trip to China*

Contents

Introduction: Why Choose this Chinese Phrase Book?

Many Chinese language textbooks are intended mainly for people who study Chinese in formal classes and are based on assumptions that are appropriate primarily for such learners. The words and phrases such textbooks introduce in early lessons are often those that help students function in a classroom setting. Such textbooks also assume that the learners' need to learn to read and write Chinese is as pressing as their need to speak it, so they introduce oral and written skills at the same rate. Underlying many such textbooks is also the assumption that they will be taught by a teacher, someone who will manage and guide the students' learning process.

However, what of people who live or work in China but do not have the opportunity to study Chinese in a formal classroom setting? Such people usually need to become "street functional" in Chinese relatively quickly, so their most pressing need is for the words and phrases that will help them deal with daily life in China. Also, during their first few trips to China, such people often have a much greater need to learn to speak and understand basic Chinese than to learn Chinese characters. Finally, such learners usually need to take charge of their language learning process, either by studying with a tutor or on their own and then going out to practice with whatever Chinese speakers they encounter.

This Chinese phrasebook is intended for this special category of Chinese learners, those people who are going to work, live or sightsee in China for an extended period but who do not have the opportunity to study in a formal Chinese language program. This book aims to meet the special needs of these learners in several ways:

1. It introduces the words, phrases, sentence patterns, and skills that are needed most often in daily life in China. The topics and content of lessons have been selected and organized to make learners functional in daily Chinese life as quickly as possible. Rather than learning how to interact socially with classmates and talk about a classroom, students learn how to buy things, ask for directions, order food in a restaurant, get assistance when something goes wrong, take buses and taxis, and so forth. Obviously, only the most basic elements of Chinese are introduced here, and learners will need to move onto other textbooks if they hope to progress beyond the initial stage, but the language tools (vocabulary, phrases, and sentence patterns) presented here are sufficient to get learners through some of the most commonly encountered situations—and also to prepare them for further Chinese study.

2. It encourages learners to make their own choices as to where to focus their efforts; especially in regards to the question of how much time and attention to devote initially to learning to read and write Chinese. Some learners will initially want to ignore Chinese characters and focus all their attention on speaking and listening. Others will want to dabble a little in characters but still invest most of their time in oral skills. Yet others will want to work on both written and spoken skills right from the start. Each unit has a core

lesson for those interested mainly in oral skills but also contains options for those who wish to begin with characters.

3. It recognizes that learners might be studying individually, with tutors, or with teachers who may have little experience teaching Chinese to foreigners (or whose ideas about teaching Chinese don't coincide with the learner's needs), and that an important part of Chinese study in such situations is learning how to work effectively with tutors who know Chinese but do not know how to teach it. In other words, learners need to learn how to gently turn well-meaning native speakers of Chinese into effective language teachers.

Underlying this book are several important assumptions:

1. It assumes that learners have different needs, interests, and learning strategies, and it is thus designed to accommodate a variety of different approaches to Chinese, especially individual decisions as to how much attention learners initially wish to devote to Chinese characters.

2. It assumes that people learn any language by first mastering that which is simple and only gradually moving into that which is more complex. As such, in the initial stages of Chinese language study, it is less important that explanations be thorough than that they are clear and easy to understand. It keeps explanations brief and relies heavily on examples to illustrate points of sentence construction and word order.

3. Finally, and most importantly, it operates under the assumption that as a language learner, you are most likely to succeed if you take charge of your learning program. In practice, this means that you need to choose the goals that are appropriate to your needs, the study methods that fit your situation and learning style, actively seek out and take advantage of opportunities to practice your Chinese, and learn how to give direction to your teachers and tutors.

Underlying each scenario in the book is a set of daily life communication problems—such as how to introduce yourself or get something to eat at a noodle stand—that you will face from your very first day traveling to China. The goal of each scenario is to provide you with the basic language tools (vocabulary, phrases, sentence patterns, and strategies) that will enable you to cope with these daily life situations using rudimentary (but ever-improving) Chinese.

Each scenario is divided into several basic sections:

Dialogue: Each piece of dialogue portrays a common daily life situation and the basic language tools and strategies you need for coping with the situation. The dialogue is presented in Pinyin and Chinese characters, and an English translation is provided for each Chinese sentence. Take note that the English translations are very literal—even to the point of being pidgin English. The danger in this is that the English translations may appear to caricature or even mock the Chinese. Please be assured that this is not at all the writer's intent; the writer has used such literal translations because their word-by-word nature preserves Chinese sentence structure and wording as much as possible, and previous learners have found that this helps them more quickly develop a feel for Chinese word order. For your reference, a more natural translation of the dialogue appears at the end of each scenario.

Vocabulary: This is a listing of all new Chinese words that are used in the dialogue and that appear elsewhere in the scenario as well as additional words that are pertinent to the topic. As much as possible, words closely related to the same topic or situation are grouped in one scenario so that they are easier to find and refer to. Occasionally, words are introduced in more than one scenario, mainly for the benefit of learners who choose to use the scenarios in an order different from the one in which they are presented in the book.

Phrases: This section presents useful short phrases relevant to the topic. Each phrase is followed by a literal English translation as well as a more natural English translation. Because of the book's title, this is the most important for you to master. You can always directly refer to this section for something you want to express in Chinese.

Notes: In each scenario, the section contains comments on new words and points of usage, which require elaboration. Here you will also find suggested strategies for dealing with daily life situations and tips on language learning.

Different Methods of Using This Chinese Phrase Book

The intent of this book is not that you work through it from beginning to end, studying all the material and doing all the exercises. Think of this book more as a menu of language material and learning methods from which you choose whatever suits your purposes. As much as possible, the material in this book has been designed and organized in such a way that it is flexible and learner-friendly, allowing you to study in a way that suits your needs and interests.

There is no end to the variety of different ways in which you could use the material in this book, but to help you get started thinking, a few basic plans are suggested:

Plan A: First Trip to China

What many people want and need during their first few trips to China are basic speaking and listening skills. Focusing your efforts on speaking and listening enables you to quickly learn how to get around China and meet your basic needs. This approach to the first stages of Chinese study also generates a lot of positive reinforcement daily because you can use what you learn and see your skills improve; also, as you speak to Chinese people, you will generally find that they are generous with praise and encouragement for foreigners who make the effort to try to learn to read and write Chinese. It might make sense to narrow your efforts to speaking and listening for a few weeks until you feel comfortable dealing with the most common daily situations.

If this sounds like the plan for you, a good strategy for using this book might be to:

> 1. Study the dialogue in each scenario, learning phrases, and sentence patterns. As you study the first few scenarios, you may also want to look at the sections of this book that introduce Chinese Pinyin, spelling, pronunciation, and tone.

> 2. Ignore the Vocabulary and Notes sections in the scenario.

> 3. Devote a lot of time to practicing speaking and listening.

Plan B: Speaking and Basic Reading

Some people want to begin studying selected Chinese characters right from the beginning of their study program, but do not want to slow down their progress in speaking and listening by investing the time it would take to learn the Chinese character for each new word they learn. Even during your first trip to China, it can be very useful to learn the most common Chinese characters found on street signs, maps, menus, and so forth in your environment. While it may be some time before you know enough characters to read all of a sign, even being able to read one or two of the characters often provides you with enough clues to determine whether or not this is the right bus, the place you are looking for, the proper bathroom door, or whatever. The other advantage of studying some Chinese characters right from the start is that as you learn to recognize a few characters, they will soon come to seem less intimidating and foreign to you; in fact, many people come to be fascinated by Chinese characters and find that learning how to read and write them becomes one of the most appealing aspects of learning Chinese.

If this plan sounds good, a suggested approach would be:

1. Follow Plan A above for speaking and listening skills.

2. Also, study the vocabulary section in each scenario. At first, you may only want to learn to recognize them, but you could also have your tutor (if you have one) point out the radicals from which most characters are constructed and perhaps show you how to write them.

3. When walking on the streets, get into the habit of looking at signs and so forth for Chinese characters that you know. This effort is not only a good way to review and memorize the characters you study in the book, but also gets you in the habit of paying attention and trying to make sense of the written Chinese in your environment; otherwise, you will probably get into the habit of simply ignoring it. You might even carry a little notebook with you for writing down new characters that look interesting or appear frequently enough to be worth learning.

Plan C: Total Mastery

If you are sure that your eventual goal is mastery of both written and spoken Chinese, you might choose to invest significant effort in developing oral and written skills right from the beginning. Making a broad frontal attack on Chinese requires a fair investment of time if you are to progress at a rate that makes you feel satisfied; for Westerners, it takes longer to learn Chinese than it does many other foreign languages—mainly because of the time investment required to learn to read and write. However, the benefit of this plan is that it will give you a good foundation for future efforts to learn to read, write, and speak Chinese.

If this plan sounds good, a suggested approach would be:

1. To study all of the material in each scenario. In particular, learn to read and write the Chinese characters in the

Dialogues and Vocabulary instead of just learning how to say them.

2. An alternative approach would be to quickly skim through this book to get your basic skills, following one of the two plans above, before starting to study with another textbook series that devotes more attention to reading. This would give you a jump-start to your study of Chinese, getting you out practicing on the streets sooner than most textbook series and programs would.

Clearly, none of these plans is the "right" plan in any universal sense, and there are endless variations on each. The right plan for you is the one that provides the best match between your goals, learning style, and the amount of time and effort you are willing to invest. Also, none of these plans are set in stone, and as you move along in your studies, you will no doubt want to set new goals and experiment with new approaches as you not only gain greater command of Chinese but also a better knowledge of what approaches to language learning work best for you.

Learning Chinese Pronunciation, Pinyin, and Tones

Westerners first learning Chinese often have the impression that it is very foreign and exotic-sounding, therefore presumably difficult to pronounce. In reality, most of the sounds used in Chinese are similar to sounds used in English and other Western languages, and most of those sounds, which are not familiar, are not very difficult to learn. There are, of course, a few exceptions to this generalization, but not many.

Chinese language books and study programs often begin with a rather long and detailed set of pronunciation exercises. Some learners find this to be a useful way to establish a foundation for later Chinese study; others find this phase of the learning process boring and not useful. The short introduction to Chinese Pinyin and pronunciation below is primarily to get you started, so the introduction below strives less for thoroughness than brevity and clarity. Little has been mentioned about sounds that are very easy or similar to English, saving effort for more challenging sounds. Ultimately, however, the best way for you to learn pronunciation is to listen to and mimic your tutor and other Chinese people. Deciding how much pronunciation drilling you need is up to you.

Chinese is a syllabic language, each word consisting of one or more short syllables. Traditionally, the Chinese consider each syllable as consisting of two parts, the initial and the final, and for the sake of convenience, the introduction below will make use of this handy division.

Initials:

b-: Pronounced like "b" in "boy"

p-: Pronounced like "p" in "pair"

m-: Pronounced like "m" in "mouse"

f-: Pronounced like "f" in "four"

d-: Pronounced like "d" in "duck"

t-: Pronounced like "t" in "tomorrow"

n-: Pronounced like "n" in "no"

l-: Pronounced like "l" in "let"

g-: Pronounced like "g" in "go"

k-: Pronounced like "k" in "king"

h-: Pronounced like "h" in "hug", but a little more guttural

y-: Pronounced like "y" in "yes"

w-: Pronounced like "w" in "we"

s-: Pronounced like "s" in "sorry"

c-: A "ts" sound, pronounced like the end of "pants"

z-: A "dz" sound, pronounced like the end of "boys"

j-: Pronounced like "j" in "jeep", but with the tongue just a little further forward

q-: Pronounced like "ch" in "chair", but with the tongue just a little further forward

---

x-: Pronounced like "sh" in "sheep", but with the tongue just a little further forward

zh-: Pronounced like "j" in "junk", but with the tongue just a little further back

ch-: Pronounced like "ch" in "cheap", but with the tongue just a little further back

sh-: Pronounced like "sh" in "ship", but with the tongue just a little further back

r-: Pronounced like "r" in "ring", but with the tongue a little higher so it buzzes ever so slightly

Finals:

-a: Pronounced like "a" in "father"

-ai: Pronounced like "y" in "why"

-ao: Pronounced like "ow" in "how"

-an: Pronounced like "an" in "fan"

-ang: Pronounced like "ung" in "hung"

-e: Pronounced like "e" in "her"

-ei: Pronounced like "ay" in "day"

-en: Pronounced like "en" in "hen"

-eng: Pronounced like "en" + "ng", no corresponding sound in English, but not difficult to make

-i: Pronounced like "ee" in "sweet" or "i" in "it" after c/z/s/ch/sh/zh/r

-ia: Pronounced like "ya" in "yard"

-ie: Pronounced like "ye" in "yes"

-iu: Pronounced like "you"

-iao: Pronounced like "y'all"

-in: Pronounced like "in"

-ing: Pronounced like "ing" in "wing"

-ian: Pronounced like "yearn" (British pronunciation)

-iang: Pronounced like "young"

-iong: Pronounced like "ong" below, but preceded by a "y"

-o: Pronounced like "wha" in "what" (British pronunciation)

-ou: Pronounced like "o" in "go" (American pronunciation)

-ong: Pronounced like "ou" + "ng", no corresponding sound in English, but not difficult to make

-u: Pronounced like "oo" in "book"

-ua: Pronounced like "oir" in "reservoir " (British pronunciation)

-ui: Pronounced like "way"

-uo: Pronounced like "woe"

-uai: Pronounced like "why"

-uan: Pronounced like "won"

-uang: Pronounced like the combination of "w" in "what" and "ung" in "hung"

-ü: Pronounced like "ew", hard to make

-ue: Pronounced like "ew" + "e" in "her", hard to make

-un: Pronounce like "ew" + "n", hard to make

er: Similar to "er" in American English, but the mouth opened a little more

wu: Pronounced like "oo" in "book"

yi: Pronounced like the letter "e"

yu: Similar to "ü"

In Chinese, the intonation of a word is an important part of its pronunciation. Generally speaking, one Chinese character corresponds to one syllable. A Chinese syllable can have no initials but must have a final and a tone. Thus, a syllable pronounced with a high intonation is a different word from the same syllable pronounced with a rising intonation, a falling-rising intonation, or a falling intonation. The classic example used to intimidate beginning learners in Chinese is the syllable "ma", which means "mother" when pronounced with a high intonation and "horse" when pronounced with a falling-rising intonation.

Westerners sometimes feel that they cannot hear tones, but this is not what the problem is. After all, speakers of English listen to and use intonation all the time. Consider the difference between a rising tone, "Yes?" (as someone answers the door) or a falling tone, "Yes!" (as an enthusiastic response to an invitation). The differences between Chinese and English is that the English intonation functions at the sentence level instead of the word level, with the rises and falls of tones, conveying the emotional impact of the sentence's message. The problem for Westerners learning Chinese is not hearing intonation per se, but hearing intonation as part of the pronunciation of a word.

The Tones of Mandarin

In Mandarin, most words are pronounced with one of four tones. Tones 1, 2, and 4 are relatively straightforward. Tone 3 changes according to the tone that follows, so will require greater elaboration:

-Tone 1:

The main vocal characteristic if the first tone is high and flat. When it is articulated, the vocal cords are tightened, and the pitch is kept at a relatively higher level for a while, like singing a long high note.

-Tone 2:

The second tone is a rising tone. It rises from the middle to a higher level while the vocal cords are gradually tightened, like the word "yes" used as a question in answering the door: "Yes?"

-Tone 3:

Usually described as a "falling-rising" tone, and this is what it sounds like when a word is pronounced in isolation or at the end of a sentence. However, you will find that if another word follows a Tone 3 word, it becomes a little cumbersome to do a complete fall + rise. Thus, one of two things will happen.

Usually, if another word follows a Tone 3 word, the rising part drops off and becomes just a low-falling tone. A good example phrase is 很快 (hěn kuài, very fast).

When one Tone 3 word is followed by another Tone 3 word, the tone of the first word changes to a rising tone just like Tone 2. Essentially, it is the initial falling part of the tone, which is now omitted. A good example phrase for this is 很好 (hěn hǎo, very good).

-Tone 4:

When it is pronounced, the vocal cords are first tightened and then relaxed. The voice hence rapidly falls from the higher to the lower level. It is relatively easy to pronounce for most people just like an enthusiastic affirmation: "Yes!"

How to Learn Tones

The natural assumption when first confronted with all these tones is that you need to memorize which tone category each new Chinese word belongs to, i.e., which word is Tone 1, Tone 2, and so forth. However, as you will quickly discover, trying to recall information in this format when you are trying to say a sentence is not very efficient; when talking, you don't have time to be constantly asking yourself "Is this word pronounced with the first or fourth tone?" It needs to come out naturally and quickly. So, what should you do?

One bit of advice is to start with your ears. When Chinese children learn to speak, nobody teaches them which words are Tone 3 and so forth. Rather, they listen and learn to say what sounds right. Likewise, to get your tones right without stopping to think before every word, you need to go with what sounds right. However, before you can do this, you need to train yourself to listen carefully to the pronunciation of new words, including their tones. For example, if you have a tutor, as your tutor pronounces new Chinese words, try to fix the intonation in your mind along with the pronunciation. Perhaps even ask your tutor to exaggerate the tone a little when pronouncing new words for you—making it funny may help you remember it better.

A second suggestion is practice, lots of it. The first few times you say anything new, it requires conscious thought, and you may well need to pause to remember which words are pronounced with which tones. However, after you have said a certain word, word combination, or phrase a few times, it starts to become automatic, and you do not need to think about it so much. Don't practice things just to the point where you can scrape your way through them once; practice until you can do them without thinking.

Finally, do not become overly concerned about tones. Yes, you should try to get them right, but you shouldn't become so worried that you are reluctant to speak. Remember: Chinese people will often understand you quite well even if your tones are wrong, especially if you speak in phrases rather than single words. For your information, if you speak in single word utterances and get the tone wrong, it may be more difficult for Chinese people to understand you, especially if the situation or context doesn't make it easy for the listener to guess what you might be trying to say. Therefore, do avoid speaking in single words! Also remember: it is much better to get a sentence out with the tones wrong than not to open your mouth at all. So long as you keep speaking—and keep paying attention to how things sound when Chinese people say them—, the accuracy of your tones and naturalness of your pronunciation will continue to improve.

Scenario 1: Exchanging Money

Dialogue

Foreigner A needs to exchange money and asks Chinese person B on the street to find out what the best place to exchange money is.

A: 请问，哪里可以换钱?

qǐng wèn, nǎ lǐ kě yǐ huàn qián?

May I ask, where possible to change money?

B: 机场、酒店和银行都可以

jī chǎng、jiǔ diàn hé yín háng dōu kě yǐ

Airport, hotel and bank, all possible

A: 哪个比较好?

nǎ gè bǐ jiào hǎo?

Which one relatively better?

B:

酒店和机场比较方便，他们肯定能讲英语。银行不太方便，但兑换率可能好一点。我也不太清楚

jiǔ diàn hé jī chǎng bǐ jiào fāng biàn, tā men kěn dìng néng jiǎng yīng yǔ. yín háng bú tài fāng biàn, dàn duì huàn lǜ kě néng hǎo yì diǎn. wǒ yě bú tài qīng chǔ

Hotel and airport relatively convenient, and they're able to speak English. Bank is not convenient, but their exchange rate is better a little. I'm not too sure

Vocabulary

换（huàn），to exchange / change

酒店（jiǔ diàn），hotel

银行（yín háng），bank

都（dōu），both / all

比较（bǐ jiào），comparatively / relatively

比（bǐ），compared to

但是（dàn shì），but

可能（kě néng），possible / possibly

方便（fāng biàn），convenient

肯定（kěn dìng），definitely

能（néng），able to

讲（jiǎng），to speak (This word is interchangeable with " 说 ")

兑换率（duì huàn lǜ），exchange rate

高（gāo），high / tall

太（tài），too (as in "too much")

清楚（qīng chǔ），clear / sure about

写（xiě），to write

贵（guì），expensive

数（shǔ），to count

Phrases

我不太清楚（wǒ bú tài qīng chǔ）

I'm not too sure

兑换率多少（duì huàn lǜ duō shǎo）？

What is the exchange rate?

请你写一下（qǐng nǐ xiě yí xià）

Please write it down

If you don't trust your ears in getting an exchange rate, this request is very useful

请你数一下（qǐng nǐ shù yí xià）

Please count it

Bank clerks may ask you to do this when handing you your money.

银行比酒店近（yín háng bǐ jiǔ diàn jìn）

The bank is closer than the hotel

他比我高（tā bǐ wǒ gāo）

He's taller than me

她比我有钱（tā bǐ wǒ yǒu qián）

She has more money than I do

哪里可以吃饭（nǎ lǐ kě yǐ chī fàn）

Where can we get something to eat?

这个西瓜贵一点（zhè gè xī guā guì yì diǎn）

This watermelon is a little more expensive

Notes

Not all banks in China exchange foreign currency. Usually, your best bet is 中国银行(zhōng guó yín háng), but sometimes you can exchange money in other banks or at the airport. You may also encounter people on the street who want to exchange money, but this is both risky and illegal.

Colloquial Translation of Dialogue

A: Excuse me, where can I exchange money?

B: Airport, hotel, and bank. All work.

A: Which is better.?

B: The hotel and airport may be more convenient, and they can surely speak English. The bank is not as convenient as the others, but their exchange rate may be a little higher, but I'm not too sure.

Scenario 2: Buying (I)

Dialogue

An important task most foreigners need to accomplish in Chinese is making a purchase. Below, A is a hesitant foreigner pointing to something in a store. B is a Chinese store clerk.

A: 这个多少钱?

zhè gè duō shao qián?

This how much money?

B: 十元

shí *yuán*

Ten Yuan

A: 那么那个多少钱?

nà me nà gè duō shao qián?

Well that how much money?

B: 五块钱

wǔ kuài qián

Five pieces of money

B: 你要不要?

nǐ yào bú yào?

You want not want?

A: 不要，谢谢

bú yào, xiè xie

Not want. Thanks

Vocabulary

钱（qián），money

你（nǐ），you

要（yào），to want

块（kuài），Chinese dollar / *yuan*

请（qǐng），please

问（wèn），to ask

这（zhè），this

再见（zài jiàn），goodbye

谢谢（xiè xie），thank you

对（duì），correct

个（gè），measure word

好（hǎo），good

早（zǎo），early / good morning

很（hěn），very

贵（guì），expensive

便宜（pián yi），cheap

多少（duō shao），how much / how many

"duō" means "many" and "shǎo" means "few". When these two are combined, "shǎo" loses its tone and become a "light tone" syllable.

不（bù），not / no

Is normally pronounced with a falling tone, but you may notice that the dialogue shows "bú", the "不" in the middle doesn't fall; rather it is pronounced with a rising tone or only a light tone. The rule is that if another fourth tone word follows "不", it becomes a rising tone.

Numbers

一（yī），one

二（èr），two

三（sān），three

四（sì），four

五（wǔ），five

六（liù），six

七（qī），seven

八（bā），eight

九（jiǔ），nine

十（shí），ten

百（bǎi），hundred

千（qiān），thousand

万（wàn），ten thousand

亿（yì），a hundred million

Phrases

你好（nǐ hǎo）？

How are you?

This is the most common Chinese greeting. To respond, simply say it back

早上/下午/晚上好（zǎo shàng / xià wǔ / wǎn shàng hǎo）

Good morning / afternoon / evening

再见（zài jiàn）

Goodbye

谢谢（xiè xie）

Thanks

这个八块钱（zhè gè bā kuài qián）

Eight *yuan* for this

In daily speech, the word "钱" is often omitted, but the measure word will normally not be omitted. Thus, for "eight *yuan*", you will often hear "bā kuài," but never "bā qián." "块" is the colloquial measure word for "元"

我要到商店买些零碎的东西（wǒ yào dào shāng diàn mǎi xiē líng suì de dōng xi）

I'll go to pick up some odds and ends at the store

你跟我去买东西吗（nǐ gēn wǒ qù mǎi dōng xi ma）？

Will you go shopping with me?

这是找你的钱（zhè shì zhǎo nǐ de qián）

Here's your change

Notes

Measure Words

In Chinese, between a number and a noun, you always need to add a measure word. A measure word is like the word "bottles" in the English phrase "four bottles of water," a word that indicates the general kind or quantity of whatever object is being discussed. The difference between English and Chinese is that whereas English only requires measure words for mass nouns, Chinese always requires a measure word between numbers and nouns. In this scenario is the measure word "kuài"; above you also see the measure word "gè" in the phrases "zhè gè" and "nà gè." You will encounter more measure words in the scenarios to come.

Tip: Listening to Chinese in real life

Listening comprehension in a foreign language involves a lot of guessing, as you will no doubt discover when you try the material in today's scenario in a real Chinese store. People don't talk like scripts in a Chinese textbook. Instead, they speak in incomplete sentences, don't always enunciate slowly and clearly, and frequently use words you haven't learned yet. Also, not everyone in China speaks standard Mandarin of the kind taught in classrooms and spoken on TV; in fact, many Chinese learn Mandarin as a second language, and their first language is some Chinese dialect that is only more or less distantly related to Mandarin.

Mandarin is the name of the Chinese dialect used as the official national language in China. It is also known as "Putonghua" because for centuries it was the language used by China's officials. "Putonghua" literally means "common language". Most Chinese speak some variant of Mandarin as their first language, and all over China, it is the language generally used in schools, the media, and most interaction between people of different regions.

The first step toward success in Chinese listening comprehension is accepting this situation as normal rather than wasting emotional energy agonizing over it. The second is developing the habit of just wading in and guessing, using any clues you have. Start by trying to hear the numbers as you ask for prices in nearby Chinese stores.

Colloquial Translation of Dialogue

A: How much does this cost?

B: Ten *yuan*

A: How about that one?

B: Five *yuan*.

B: Do you want it?

A: No thank you.

Scenario 3: Buying (II)

Dialogue:

Emboldened by the success of the visit in Scenario 2, A has returned to the Chinese store for another purchase. B is still the clerk.

A: 有没有啤酒?

yǒu méi yǒu pí jiǔ?

Have not have beer?

B: 有，要几瓶?

Yǒu, yào jǐ píng?

Have. Want how many bottles?

A: 三瓶。有没有雪茄?

sān píng. yǒu méi yǒu xuě jiā?

Three bottles. Have not have cigars?

B:对不起，没有

duì bù qǐ, méi yǒu

Sorry, not have

A: 好吧，三瓶啤酒多少钱？

hǎo ba, sān píng pí jiǔ duō shǎo qián?

Well, three bottles of beer how much money?

B: 五元一瓶，一共十五块

wǔ yuán yì píng, yí gòng shí wǔ kuài

Five *yuan* one bottle; fifteen *yuan* in total

Vocabulary

有（yǒu），have

没有（méi yǒu），not have

啤酒（pí jiǔ），beer

雪茄（xuě jiā），cigar

几（jǐ），several / how many

对不起（duì bù qǐ），sorry / excuse me

意思（yì sī），meaning

肥皂（féi zào），soap

牙膏（yá gāo），toothpaste

笔（bǐ），pen

卫生纸（wèi shēng zhǐ），toilet paper

洗发水（xǐ fà shuǐ），shampoo

饮料（yǐn liào），beverage

零食（líng shí），snack

Phrases

什么意思（shén me yì sī）?

What does it mean?

"雪茄"是什么意思（"xuě jiā" shì shén me yì sī）?

What does "cigar" mean?

糖多少钱（táng duō shǎo qián）?

How much for the sugar?

有没有糖（yǒu méi yǒu táng）?

Do you have any sugar?

This "有没有" construction is used where in English you would say "Do you have any _____?" or "Are there any _____?" It also has other uses: "你有没有吃饭 (nǐ yǒu méi yǒu chī fàn)?" is one way to say, "Have you eaten?"

打扰一下，你能告诉我雪茄在哪儿卖吗（dǎ rǎo yí xià, nǐ néng gào sù wǒ xuě qié zài nǎ ér mài ma）?

Excuse me, could you tell me where I can get some cigars?

我能看看这块表吗（wǒ néng kàn kan zhè kuài biǎo ma）?

May I have a look at the watch?

Notes

Strategy: Reading Chinese on the street

Reading, like listening, is a guessing game in which you will need to use whatever clues you have to get the information you need. You won't be reading Chinese novels anytime soon, but you can already start using the characters you know to unlock the secrets of Chinese maps, signs, menus, and so forth. If you get into the habit of looking at the written Chinese around you in daily life, you will not only review the characters you already know but also notice new ones that appear frequently and beg you to learn them. Carry a little notebook so you can copy down characters you want to learn.

Colloquial Translation of Dialogue

A: Do you have any beer?

B: Yes, how many bottles do you want?

A: Three. Do you have any cigars?

B: Sorry, we don't.

A: Well, how much for three bottles of beer?

B: Five yuan each, fifteen in total.

Scenario 4: Buying (III)

Dialogue

In some Chinese shops, goods are behind a counter and you will need to ask a clerk to get the item for you. A is attempting to make a rather mundane purchase in such a shop.

A: 你们这儿有没有毛巾?

nǐ men zhè ér yǒu méi yǒu máo jīn?

You here have not have towels?

B: 有，你要什么颜色?

yǒu, nǐ yào shén me yán sè?

Have. You want what color?

A: 我要红色的

wǒ yào hóng sè de

I want a red-colored one

B: 我们有大的和小的。你要什么样的?

wǒ men yǒu dà de hé xiǎo de. nǐ yào shén me yàng de?

We have big ones and small ones. You want what kind?

A: 麻烦你给我看看那个大的

má fán nǐ gěi wǒ kàn kan nà gè dà de

Trouble you give me look at that big one

B: 哪个?

nǎ gè?

Which one?

A: 对!那个!

Duì! nà gè!

Right! That!

Vocabulary

这儿（zhè ér），here

毛巾（máo jīn），towel

颜色（yán sè），color

大（dà），big

小（xiǎo），small

什么样（shén me yàng），what kind

麻烦（má fan），trouble / to trouble

给（gěi），give

对（duì），right / correct

那个（nà gè），that

商场（shāng chǎng），mall

公司（gōng sī），company

大厦（dà shà），building

百货大楼（bǎi huò dà lóu），department store

超市（chāo shì），supermarket

购物广场（gòu wù guǎng chǎng），plaza

衬衫（chèn shān），shirt

裙子（qún zi），skirt

外套（wài tào），coat

鞋子（xié zi），shoes

毛衣（máo yī），sweater

裤子（kù zi），pants

内衣（nèi yī），underwear

袜子（wà zi），socks

新（xīn），new

长（cháng），long

宽（kuān），wide / broad

旧（jiù），old

短（duǎn），short

窄（zhǎi），narrow

浅（qiǎn），shallow

深（shēn），deep

红（hóng），red

橙（chéng）, orange

黄（huáng）, yellow

绿（lǜ）, green

蓝（lán）, blue

紫（zǐ）, purple

黑（hēi）, black

白（bái）, white

灰（huī）, grew

Phrases

麻烦你给我那条毛巾（má fan nǐ gěi wǒ nà tiáo máo jīn）?

May I bother you to give me that towel?

还有别的颜色吗（hái yǒu bié de yán sè ma）?

Do you have another color?

有没有更好的（yǒu méi yǒu gèng hǎo de）?

Do you have a better one?

这个太小了，有大点的吗（zhè gè tài xiǎo le, yǒu dà diǎn de ma）?

This is too small for me, do you have a bigger one?

你穿多大号的（nǐ chuān duō dà hào de）?

What's your size?

它特别适合你（tā tè bié shì hé nǐ）

It suits you very much

能换一个吗（néng huàn yí gè ma）?

Can you show me another one?

麻烦你开门（má fan nǐ kāi mén）？

Can I trouble you to open the door?

我要那件紫色的裙子（wǒ yào nà jiàn zǐ sè de qún zi）

I want that purple skirt

这件衬衫真好看（zhè jiàn chèn shān zhēn hǎo kàn）

This shirt looks nice

我喜欢这条裤子（wǒ xǐ huān zhè tiáo kù zi）

I like these pants

能试一试吗（néng shì yí shì ma）？

Can I try them on?

对我来说太贵了（duì wǒ lái shuō tài guì le）

It's too expensive for me

我要了（wǒ yào le）

I'll take it

我该付多少钱（wǒ gāi fù duō shǎo qián）？

How much do I owe you?

Notes

Plurals

Chinese makes no distinction between the singular and plural forms of most nouns. For example, "门 (mén)" means both "door" and "doors". Whether or not something is singular or plural is determined from context.

-er ending

In Northern China, an -er ending is added to many words. For example, while Southern Chinese would say, "这里 (zhè lǐ)," northerners would say, "这儿 (zhè ér)." Both mean "here". You need to decide if you want to follow Northern or Southern custom or learn to switch depending on your audience, but for now, focus on not getting too confused by these reginal variations when you listen.

Tip: Tones

At the early stages of Chinese study and use you may make quite a few tonal mistakes when you speak. Generally, a tonal mistake in the context of a sentence won't confuse a Chinese speaker too much, but if you speak in isolated words and get the tones wrong, speakers may not understand you. One strategy for minimizing tones as a communication problem is to create context by using complete phrases or sentences—or lots of body language.

Colloquial Translation of Dialogue

A: Do you have any towels here?

B: Yes, what color would you like?

A: Red.

B: We have big ones and little ones, what kind do you want?

A: Could you let me have a look at that big one?

B: Which one?

A: Yeah, that one!

Scenario 5: Drinks and Snacks

Dialogue

A and B are hungry / thirsty foreigners passing a local general store. C is the store clerk.

A: 我饿了。你呢？

wǒ è le, nǐ ne

I hungry. You?

B: 我不饿，但是有一点渴

wǒ bú è, dàn shì yǒu yì diǎn kě

I not hungry, but a little thirsty

A: 你有没有饼干？

nǐ yǒu méi yǒu bǐng gān?

You have not have cookies?

C: 有。你要哪种？

Yǒu. nǐ yào nǎ zhǒng?

Have. You want which kind?

A: 那种是甜的还是咸的?

nà zhǒng shì tián de hái shì xián de?

That kind is sweet or salty?

C: 这种是巧克力的

zhè zhǒng shì qiǎo kè lì de

This kind is chocolate

B: 我要一个可乐

wǒ yào yí gè kě lè

I want a cola

C: 大瓶还是小瓶?

dà píng hái shì xiǎo píng?

Big bottle or small bottle?

B: 我要罐装的

wǒ yào guàn zhuāng de

I want can filled

Vocabulary

饿（è），hungry

渴（kě），thirsty

巧克力（qiǎo kè lì），chocolate

饼干（bǐng gān），crackers / cookies

可乐（kě lè），cola / coke

瓶（píng），bottle

种（zhǒng），kind / type

罐（guàn），can

还是（hái shì），or

甜（tián），sweet

咸（xián），salty

装（zhuāng），to fill / to install

酸（suān），sour

辣（là），hot / spicy

喝（hē），to drink

面包（miàn bāo），bread

冰淇淋（bīng qí lín），ice cream

杯子（bēi zi），cup

罐头（guàn tou），can food

干（gān），dry

汽水（qì shuǐ），soda

咖啡（kā fēi），coffee

茶（chá），tea

水（shuǐ），water

开水（kāi shuǐ），boiled water

冰水（bīng shuǐ），ice water

白酒（bái jiǔ），Chinese liquor

果汁（guǒ zhī），juice

牛奶（niú nǎi），milk

葡萄酒（pú táo jiǔ），wine

矿泉水（kuàng quán shuǐ），mineral water

Phrases

我有点饿（wǒ yǒu diǎn è）

I'm a little hungry

这儿有点儿冷（zhè ér yǒu diǎn ér lěng）

It's a little cold here

我要那个大的（wǒ yào nà gè dà de）

I want that big one

她想买酸的（tā xiǎng mǎi suān de）

She wants to buy the sour kind

你想吃面包还是饼干（nǐ xiǎng chī miàn bāo hái shì bǐng gān）?

Do want to eat bread or crackers?

这是甜的还是咸的（zhè shì tián de hái shì xián de）?

Is this sweet or salty?

你要大的还是小的（nǐ yào dà de hái shì xiǎo de）?

Do you want a big one or a small one?

Notes

Tip: Finding time

One of the greatest problems that learners outside formal language study programs face is a shortage of time, and usually, an abundance of other things need to be done. Usually, to sustain even a modest study program, you need to regularly block out a portion of prime time in your daily schedule (i.e., time when you are reasonably alert) to devote to study, and generally, this means making sacrifices in some other area of your life. Attempts to learn a language without allocating adequate time to the task typically result in more frustration than progress. In contrast, even if you can only find half an hour of quality time each day for Chinese study, you will be able to make gradual but genuine progress.

Colloquial Translation of Dialogue

A: I'm hungry. How about you?

B: I'm not hungry, but I'm a little thirsty.

A: Do you have any cookies?

C: Yes, what kind do you want?

A: Is that kind sweet or salty?

C: This kind is chocolate.

B: I want a cola.

C: Big or small bottle?

B: I want a can.

Scenario 6: In the Cafeteria

Dialogue

A is a curious and hungry foreigner looking at food in a Chinese cafeteria. B, the Chinese server, patiently answers questions.

A: 这是什么?

zhè shì shén me?

This is what?

B: 这是炸鸡

zhè shì zhá jī

This is fried chicken

A: 那个呢?

nà gè ne?

Then that?

B: 炸鱼。要来一份吗?

zhá yú. yào lái yí fèn ma?

Fried fish. Want one?

A: 可以

kě yǐ

Sure

B: 你的汉语还不错

nǐ de hàn yǔ hái bú cuò

Your Chinese not bad

A: 哪里哪里

nǎ lǐ nǎ lǐ

Where, where

Vocabulary

这（zhè），this

是（shì），is

什么（shén me），what

The "n" in this word is silent. This is one of the very few Chinese words not pronounced exactly as the Pinyin spelling would indicate.

鸡（jī），chicken

鸡肉（jī ròu），chicken meat

鱼（yú），fish

吃（chī），to eat

的（de），possessive marker

吗（ma），question marker

汉语（hàn yǔ），Chinese language

哪里（nǎ lǐ），where

听（tīng），to listen

懂（dǒng），to understand

肉（ròu），meat

猪（zhū），pig

猪肉（zhū ròu），pork

羊（yáng），sheep / goat

羊肉（yáng ròu），mutton

牛（niú），cow / bull

牛肉（niú ròu），beef

Phrases

这是什么?（zhè shì shén me）

What is this?

Notice that the word order for this question is the opposite of the order in English, and that the same word order is used for both question and answer

这是猪肉吗?（zhè shì zhū ròu ma）

Is this pork?

你要点菜了吗?（nǐ yào diǎn cài le ma）

Are you ready to order?

你要什么甜点?（nǐ yào shén me tián diǎn）

What would you like for dessert?

这是你的吗?（zhè shì nǐ de ma）

Is this yours?

咸不咸?（xián bú xián）

Salty or not?

甜不甜？（tián bú tián）

Sweet or not?

辣不辣？（là bú là）

Spicy or not?

我听不懂（wǒ tīng bù dǒng）

I don't understand

好吃（hǎo chī）

Tastes good

不好吃（bù hǎo chī）

Tastes bad

我能用支票或信用卡吗？（wǒ néng yòng zhī piào huò xìn yòng kǎ ma）

Can I pay by check or credit card?

对不起，我们只收现金（duì bù qǐ, wǒ men zhī shōu xiàn jīn）

Sorry, we only accept cash

Notes

In the previous scenario, you saw that a measure word is required between numbers and nouns. In the dialogue above, you see that a measure word is also usually required after "这".

个 (gè)

This is the most common measure word in Chinese, and when you are in doubt as to what measure word to use, you can simply use "gè".

呢 (ne)

A question marker, but it is only used for brief follow-up questions in situations where context already makes the question clear. So, for example, instead of asking the whole question "这是什么(zhè shì shén me)?" several times in a row as you point to different items in a store or restaurant, for the follow-up questions you could ask, "这个呢 (zhè gè ne)?" and "那个呢 (nà gè ne)?"

的 (de)

Can mark possession, like so:

-我的 (wǒ de), my/mine

-你的 (nǐ de), your/yours

-他/她的 (tā de), his/hers

哪里哪里 (nǎ lǐ nǎ lǐ)

The normal polite Chinese response to a compliment is to deny it, and this is often done with this phrase, which literally means "where, where?" but would better be translated something like "Not at all".

Strategy: Controlling conversations with questions

In early stages of Chinese practice in real life, a good way to give yourself a fighting chance to understand what Chinese speakers say is by controlling the conversation with questions that help you predict what you might hear in response. "这是什么 (zhè shì shén me)?" is a very useful question because it both generates predictable responses and new vocabulary. Yes/no questions are also good because they limit the possible responses.

Tip: Grammar

Learning Chinese grammar is largely a question of remembering word order. This is the main reason why Chinese word order is preserved as much as possible in the English translation of the dialogue sentences, even when the result is pidgin English. For example, note that the word order in "这是什么 (zhè shì shén me)?" is the opposite of the English "What is this?"

Colloquial Translation of Dialogue

A: What is this?

B: Fried chicken.

A: What about that?

B: Fried fish, do you want some?

A: Sure.

B: Your Chinese isn't bad.

A: Thank you.

Scenario 7: The Noodle Stand

Dialogue

Foreigner B is ordering a meal at a small Chinese noodle stand. A is the Chinese owner.

A: 你想吃什么?

nǐ xiǎng chī shén me?

You want to eat what?

B: 等一下，我看一下菜单。好，我来一碗面条

děng yí xià, wǒ kàn yí xià cài dān. hǎo, wǒ lái yì wǎn miàn tiáo

Wait a minute, I look a moment menu. Okay, I take one bowl noodles

A: 好的，你还要吃什么?喜欢吃水饺吗?

hǎo de, nǐ hái yào chī shén me? xǐ huān chī shuǐ jiǎo ma?

Okay. You also want to eat what? Like to eat dumpling?

B: 很喜欢，那再要一盘水饺吧

hěn xǐ huān, nà zài yào yì pán shuǐ jiǎo ba

Very much, then also want a plate dumpling

Vocabulary

等（děng），to wait

一下（yí xià），a moment

菜单（cài dān），menu

来（lái），to come / to take

碗（wǎn），bowl / a bowl of

面条（miàn tiáo），noodles

喜欢（xǐ huān），to like

也（yě），also

水饺（shuǐ jiǎo），dumpling

碟（dié），plate / a plate of

用（yòng），to use

菜（cài），dishes / food

筷子（kuài zi），chopsticks

结账（jié zhàng），to count up a bill

走（zǒu），to walk / to leave

炒饭（chǎo fàn），fried rice

馒头（mán tou），steamed bread

包子（bāo zi），steamed bread with filling

煎饼（jiān bing），fried flatbread

烧饼（shāo bing），baked flatbread

油条（yóu tiáo），deep fried breadsticks

Phrases

我要结账（wǒ yào jié zhàng）

Please get me the bill

来一碗面条怎么样（lái yì wǎn miàn tiáo zěn me yàng）？

How about having a bowl of noodles?

很喜欢（hěn xǐ huān）

Note the word order in this phrase. The "很" comes before "喜欢"，unlike word order in English

Very like

Questions you will often hear in a restaurant:

你会不会用筷子（nǐ huì bú huì yòng kuài zi）？

Can you use chopsticks?

你喜欢中国菜吗（nǐ xǐ huān zhōng guó cài ma）？

Do you like Chinese food?

需要给你一套刀叉吗（xū yào gěi nǐ yí tào dāo chā ma）？

Do you need a knife and a fork?

你快一点（nǐ kuài yì diǎn）！

Hurry up!

请等一下（qǐng děng yí xià）

Please wait a moment

我们来两碗面和三个包子（wǒ men lái liǎng wǎn miàn hé sān gè bāo zi）

We'll take two bowls of noodles and three steamed buns

Notes

Tip: Accents and dialects

One frustration of learning Chinese for average people instead of language teachers is that not all people use standard Chinese pronunciation. In fact, there are only a few places in China where the average person pronounces things the way textbooks say they should. Furthermore, in many provinces, Chinese people speak a dialect and only learn Mandarin as a second language.

First, accept this as reality rather than burning a lot of emotional energy getting frustrated by it. Perhaps even revel in it as a reflection of China's rich regional diversity. Second, get used to guessing; the sentence that sounded vaguely like "你好" might actually have been "你好", albeit with a heavy local accent. Third, learn a few words in the local dialect. You will probably get all kinds of brownie points with local people for knowing a few of their words.

Colloquial Translation of Dialogue

A: What do you want to eat?

B: Wait a minute. I'll take a look at the menu. Okay. I'll have a bowl of noodles.

A: Okay. What else do you want to have? Do you like dumplings?

B: Yes, I like dumplings a lot. I'd also like a plate of dumplings.

Scenario 8: In the Restaurant

Dialogue

Foreigner B and their friend have been emboldened by earlier success with noodles and try ordering a more sophisticated meal at a local restaurant. A is the eager waitress.

A: 你们吃什么菜?

nǐ men chī shén me cài?

You eat what dishes?

B: 有什么好吃的?

yǒu shén me hǎo chī de?

Have what good to eat?

A: 烤虾, 行不行?

kǎo xiā, xíng bú xíng?

Baked shrimp, okay not okay?

B: 请给我看看菜单。烤虾太贵了，还有别的吗?

qǐng gěi wǒ kàn kan cài dān. kǎo xiā tài guì le, hái yǒu bié de ma?

Please give me look at menu. Baked shrimp too expensive. Also have other?

A: 青椒肉片，怎么样？

qīng jiāo ròu piàn, zěn me yàng?

Green pepper with pork slices, what about it?

B: 好。我们再来一个青菜、一碗酸辣汤和两碗米饭

hǎo. wǒ men zài lái yí gè qīng cài, yì wǎn suān là tāng hé liǎng wǎn mǐ fàn

Alright. We also want a green vegetable dish, a bowl of hot-sour soup, and two bowls of rice

Vocabulary

虾（xiā），shrimp

烤（kǎo），bake

酸辣（suān là），sour-hot

米饭（mǐ fàn），cooked rice

行（xíng），okay

别的（bié de），other

肉片（ròu piàn），meet slices

青椒（qīng jiāo），green pepper

青菜（qīng cài），greens

汤（tāng），soup

怎么样（zěn me yàng），how about

味精（wèi jīng），MSG

饱（bǎo），full

蔬菜（shū cài），vegetables

海鲜（hǎi xiān），seafood

汤匙（tāng chí），spoon

勺子（sháo zi），ladle

酱油（jiàng yóu），soy sauce

油（yóu），oil

醋（cù），vinegar

盐（yán），salt

糖（táng），sugar

蒜（suàn），garlic

辣椒酱（là jiāo jiàng），hot sauce

Some Chinese dishes beloved by foreigners:

蛋花汤（dàn huā tāng），egg flower soup

酸辣汤（suān là tāng），sour-hot soup

麻婆豆腐（má pó dòu fu），spicy bean curd

鱼香肉丝（yú xiāng ròu sī），spicy pork threads

鱼香茄子（yú xiāng qié zi），spicy eggplant

糖醋里脊（táng cù lǐ jǐ），sweet sour pork

家常豆腐（jiā cháng dòu fu），home-style tofu

宫保鸡丁（gōng bǎo jī dīng），Kong Bao chicken

腰果鸡丁（yāo guǒ jī dīng），cashew chicken

红烧牛肉（hóng shāo niú ròu），braised beef

西红柿炒蛋（xī hóng shì chǎo dàn），tomato scrambled eggs

苦瓜炒蛋（kǔ guā chǎo dàn），bitter melon scrambled eggs

炒青菜（chǎo qīng cài），fried green vegetables

干煸四季豆（gān biān sì jì dòu），fried full season beans

炒空心菜（chǎo kōng xīn cài），fried leafy vegetable

油炸土豆条（yóu zhà tǔ dòu tiáo），fried potato threads

拔丝地瓜（bá sī dì guā），candied sweet potato

Phrases

不要放味精（bú yào fàng wèi jīng）

No MSG

干杯!（gān bēi）

Bottoms up!

我吃饱了（wǒ chī bǎo le）

I'm full

我自己来（wǒ zì jǐ lái）

I can do it by myself

Useful when a host insists on putting food in your bowl for you—perhaps things you don't want. You may feel uncomfortable with this kind of behavior, especially if someone is doing this with their own chopsticks, but this is indeed a Chinese way of showing hospitality

够了（gòu le）

It's enough

This is useful when a zealous host heaps too much food into your bowl

你想吃什么？（nǐ xiǎng chī shén me）

What do you want to eat?

有沙拉吗？（yǒu shā lā ma）

Is there any salad?

这里面是什么？（zhè lǐ miàn shì shén me）

What's in this dish?

我要这个（wǒ yào zhè gè）

I want this

给我两碗米饭（gěi wǒ liǎng wǎn mǐ fàn）

Two bowls of rice, please

米饭和菜一起上（mǐ fàn hé cài yì qǐ shàng）

Please bring the rice and dish together

还要些什么？（hái yào xiē shén me）

What else do you want?

就要这些（jiù yào zhè xiē）

These will be enough

不要了（bú yào le）

Nothing else

我们不吃螃蟹（wǒ men bù chī páng xiè）

We don't like to eat crab

再来一瓶果汁（zài lái yì píng guǒ zhī）

A cup of juice, please

我要买单（wǒ yào mǎi dān）

I'll pay the bill

我们要发票和收据（wǒ men yào fā piào hé shōu jù）

We want the receipt and invoice

可以打包吗？（kě yǐ dǎ bāo ma）

Can we pack the remaining food?

Notes

Strategy: Ordering in a restaurant

If you know what you want and how to say what you want, there will not be a problem. However, this is often not the case, so the dialogue above models a coping strategy. Ask the waiter/waitress to recommend something, but most places will recommend their best and most expensive dishes. Therefore, check what they recommend on the menu to ensure that it isn't beyond your means. Remember: ask before ordering a dish that has no price listed next to it—they are usually the expensive delicacies.

Tip: Memorizing vocabulary

Learning a new language requires memorizing lots of vocabulary, so you need to develop good strategies for embedding many new words in your memory. Some suggestions:

- *Repetition*: The more times you see, hear, say, write a word, the more likely you are to remember it.

- *Concentration*: Staying alert when you memorize is vitally important.

- *Application*: A word that you find a chance to use in a conversation is more likely to stay with you than one you only study in a book.

- *Movement*: Physical movement combined with memorization helps you remember words better. Sway your arms, rock your head, pace the room, do whatever you need to.

- *Associations*: Associate a word with something memorable, funny, shocking, etc. It may help to associate the Chinese word with some word in your own language that the Chinese word sounds like—the more absurd, the better.

Colloquial Translation of Dialogue

A: What would you like to eat?

B: What's good?

A: How about baked shrimp?

B: Please let me look at the menu. Shrimp is too expensive, do you have anything else?

A: How about green pepper with pork slices?

B: Okay. We'll also take a dish of greens, a bowl of hot-sour soup, and two bowls of rice.

Scenario 9: In the Market

Dialogue

Foreigner A is in a market. B is a well-supplied fruit vendor.

A: 这水果新鲜吗？

zhè shuǐ guǒ xīn xiān ma?

This fruit fresh?

B: 很新鲜。要买多少？

hěn xīn xiān. yào mǎi duō shǎo?

Very fresh. Want buy how much?

A: 西瓜多少钱一斤？

xī guā duō shǎo qián yì jīn?

Watermelon per catty how much?

B: 五块六一斤。要几斤？

wǔ kuài liù yì jīn. yào jǐ jīn?

One catty 5.6 yuan. Want how many catties?

A: 十块钱两斤，好不好？

shí kuài qián liǎng jīn, hǎo bú hǎo?

Two catties 10 yuan. Okay not okay?

B: 行，行

xíng, xíng

Okay, okay

Vocabulary

水果（shuǐ guǒ）， fruit

西瓜（xī guā）， watermelon

新鲜（xīn xian）， fresh

斤（jīn）， catty / half-kilo

两（liǎng）， tenth of a catty

公斤（gōng jīn）， kilogram

半（bàn）， half

苹果（píng guǒ）， apple

香蕉（xiāng jiāo）， banana

梨（lí）， pear

桃子（táo zi）， peach

橙子（chéng zi）， orange

胡萝卜（hú luó bo）， carrot

白萝卜（bái luó bo）， turnip

葱（cōng）， green onion

洋葱（yáng cōng）， onion

菜花（cài huā）， cauliflower

白菜（bái cài），cabbage

Phrases

便宜一点，行不行？（pián yi yì diǎn, xíng bù xíng）

Can it be cheaper?

太贵了！（tài guì le）

Too expensive!

有点贵（yǒu diǎn guì）

A bit expensive

五块钱，卖不卖？（wǔ kuài qián, mài bú mài）

How about five *yuan*?

这个水果坏了（zhè gè shuǐ guǒ huài le）

This fruit has gone bad

香蕉三斤多少钱？（xiāng jiāo sān jīn duō shǎo qián）

How much for 3 catty banana?

西瓜多少钱一斤？（xī guā duō shǎo qián yì jīn）

How much is watermelon per catty?

两块六一斤（liǎng kuài liù yì jīn）

2.6 *yuan* per catty

Notes

The main traditional weight measurement used in Chinese markets is the "斤(jīn)". This is about half a kilogram or a little more than a pound. A "两(liǎng)" is a tenth of a "斤". These are the measurements most often used in markets for buying food. Metric weights, however, are also commonly used in Chinese markets. The word for kilogram in Chinese is "公斤(gōng jīn)".

Strategy: Bargaining in markets

Foreigners sometimes avoid Chinese markets because sentences fly around too fast, and they might worry about being cheated. However, there are several good reasons to become "market literate". First, there is a lot of good food in markets. Second, markets are a great free language class where you can practice much of your most basic language tools. Third, bargaining is fun once you have done it a few times and learned the ropes. Finally, having a few vendors at the market who recognize you is a wonderful boost to your sense that you are becoming a part of "life" when you are in China.

You can often bargain at markets or with street vendors, although usually, the price won't go down too far. Here are some suggestions:

- Try to find out roughly what price something should be before you go to the market so that you know if the quoted price is outrageous. Remember: the quoted prices vary by the season and even by the day, so to get good information you need to ask someone who shops in the market often.

- Basic bargaining moves include asking for a cheaper price or making a counter-offer.

- If you are buying more than one item, a good strategy is to offer the vendor a rounded price that is slightly lower than the original total amount.

- If the purchase is not vital to you, you can always try walking away. You may get called back with a better offer, but not always.

- Finally, become a regular customer, and you will probably get a good price right off the bat.

Colloquial Translation of Dialogue

A: Is this fruit fresh?

B: Very fresh. How much do you want to buy?

A: How much is watermelon per catty?

B: 5.6 *yuan* per catty.

A: How about two catties for 10 *yuan*?

B: Okay, okay.

Scenario 10: In the Bookstore

Dialogue

B wants to make a purchase in a bookstore. A is the Chinese clerk.

A: 你想买什么?

nǐ xiǎng mǎi shén me?

You want to buy what?

B: 我想买几本书

wǒ xiǎng mǎi jǐ běn shū

I want to buy several books

A: 什么样的书?

shén me yàng de shū?

What kind of books?

B: 有没有汉语课本?

yǒu méi yǒu hàn yǔ kè běn?

Have not have Chinese textbooks?

A: 没有。你还要什么?

méi yǒu. nǐ hái yào shén me

Not have. You still want what?

B: 汉英词典有没有?

hàn yīng cí diǎn yǒu méi yǒu?

Chinese-English dictionary have or not?

A: 有。还有吗?

yǒu. hái yǒu ma?

Have. What else?

B: 一本中国历史书

yì běn zhōng guó lì shǐ shū

A Chinese history book

Vocabulary

想（xiǎng）, want to

本（běn）, measure word for books

课本（kè běn）, textbook

还（hái）, still / else

汉英（hàn yīng）, Chinese-English

词典（cí diǎn）, dictionary

张（zhāng）, measure word for photos / maps / papers

历史（lì shǐ）, history

政治（zhèng zhì）, politic

经济（jīng jì）, economy

文化（wén huà），culture

数学（shù xué），math

物理（wù lǐ），physics

化学（huà xué），chemistry

生物（shēng wù），biology

地理（dì lǐ），geography

文学（wén xué），literature

中国文学（zhōng guó wén xué），Chinese literature

外国文学（wài guó wén xué），foreign literature

文具（wén jù），stationary, pen, etc

地图（dì tú），map

小说（xiǎo shuō），novel / fiction

Phrases

还有呢（hái yǒu ne）？

What else?

你想看书吗（nǐ xiǎng kàn shū ma）？

Do you want to read?

我想坐在这（wǒ xiǎng zuò zài zhè）

I want to sit here

有没有汉英词典（yǒu méi yǒu hàn yīng cí diǎn）？

Do you have any Chinese-English dictionaries?

地图有没有（dì tú yǒu méi yǒu）？

Do you have any maps?

Notes

Chinese word order:

Chinese word order is sometimes flexible, especially in spoken Chinese. Note that in the dialogue above, "有没有" can come before the subject or after. In your speaking, you might initially choose to stick with one pattern, but expect to hear Chinese people vary the pattern.

Chinese dictionaries:

When getting a dictionary for studying Chinese, choose one with many example phrases and sentences so you can learn word usage as well as meaning. Examples also give you good clues as to connotations, level of formality, and so forth.

Colloquial Translation of Dialogue

A: What do you want to buy?

B: I want to buy some books.

A: What kind of books?

B: Do you have any Chinese textbooks?

A: No, we don't. Was there anything else that you want?

B: Do you have any Chinese-English dictionaries?

A: We do, anything else?

B: One Chinese history book.

Scenario 11: Taking the Taxi

Dialogue

Foreigner A is headed to the museum and waves down a taxi; B is the taxi driver.

B: 去哪里？

qù nǎ lǐ?

Go to where?

A: 到博物馆。请打表

dào bó wù guǎn. qǐng dǎ biǎo

To museum. Please start meter

A: 请停车

qǐng tíng chē

Please stop the taxi

B: 这儿不可以停车。我在前面停吧

zhè ér bù kě yǐ tíng chē. wǒ zài qián miàn tíng ba

Here not permitted stop taxi. I at ahead stop car, how's that?

A: 好吧

hǎo ba

Okay

Vocabulary

博物馆（bó wù guǎn）, museum

医院（yī yuàn）, hospital

公安局（gōng ān jú）, police office

汽车站（qì chē zhàn）, bus stop

飞机场（fēi jī chǎng）, airport

火车站（huǒ chē zhàn）, train station

公园（gōng yuán）, park

游乐园（yóu lè yuán）, amusement part

海边（hǎi biān）, seaside

停（tíng）, to stop

打表（dǎ biǎo）, to start a meter

抽烟（chōu yān）, to smoke

拐弯（guǎi wān）, to turn

路（lù）, road

高速公路（gāo sù gōng lù）, highway

走（zǒu）, to walk / to go / to leave

出租车/的士/计程车（chū zū chē / dī shì / jì chéng chē）, taxi

公交车（gōng jiāo chē）, bus

自行车（zì xíng chē），bike

摩托车（mó tuō chē），motorcycle

Phrases

你要去哪里（nǐ yào qù nǎ lǐ）？

Where are you going?

打不打表（dǎ bù dǎ biǎo）?

Do you have a meter?

This is a good question not only for checking to see if a vehicle has a meter—and is thus a legal taxi—but also for suggesting that the meter be used

请开一下后备箱（qǐng kāi yí xià hòu bèi xiāng）

Please open the trunk

你知道怎么去超市吗（nǐ zhī dào zěn me qù chāo shì ma）？

Do you know how to get to the supermarket?

看表吧（kàn biǎo ba）?

Let's go according to the meter price, okay?

This is useful if a taxi driver starts trying to negotiate a price instead of using the meter

你能停一下吗nǐ néng tíng yí xià ma）？

Can you stop for a minute?

你能等我十分钟吗（nǐ néng děng wǒ shí fèn zhōng ma）？

Can you wait for me for like ten minutes?

到机场多少钱（dào jī chǎng duō shǎo qián）?

How much to the airport?

This is used when you want to negotiate a price

我到了（wǒ dào le）!

I'm there!

这儿可以停车（zhè ér kě yǐ tíng chē）

It's permitted to stop the vehicle here

在图书馆不可以抽烟（zài tú shū guǎn bù kě yǐ chōu yān）

You are not allowed to smoke in the library

我们走吧（wǒ men zǒu ba）

Let's leave

我们明天去公园吧（wǒ men míng tiān qù gōng yuán ba）

Let's go to the park tomorrow

Notes

车（chē）

In Chinese, the word "车" is used much more often than the word "vehicle" is in English. In fact, whereas in English one usually says "car," "bus," or whatever, in Chinese, the more general word "车" is often used, with context clarifying what kind of vehicle is in question.

Strategy: Negotiating taxis

Your ability to get around Chinese cities expands dramatically once you become comfortable using Chinese taxis, so this is a skill worth developing as soon as possible. In general, you don't need to worry much about taxi drivers overcharging you in China, but there are always a few exceptions, and it would be too bad if concern for being overcharged were to cause you to avoid taxis. A few suggestions for minimizing problems:

- Taxis with meters are less likely to overcharge than those which lack meters.

- It is better to get a taxi at a regular taxi stand or to hail one on the street than it is to go with a taxi driver who hustles business at places like a train and bus station. These locations generally have a regular taxi stand, though you may need to look for it. If you can't find one, you might want to walk a little distance from the station before hailing a taxi.

- For more distant destinations, such as airports, taxis often don't charge according to the meter. For these destinations, it is especially important to find out in advance what would be a fair price according to local custom.

Colloquial Translation of Dialogue

A: Where are you going?

B: To the museum, please use the meter.

B: Please stop the taxi.

A: I can't stop here. I'll stop up ahead, okay?

A: Sure.

Scenario 12: On the Train

Dialogue

Foreigner A is at a train station trying to buy a ticket to Shanghai but isn't sure which is the right ticket window. B is the ticket seller.

A: 这儿有没有到上海的火车票?

zhè ér yǒu méi yǒu dào shàng hǎi de huǒ chē piào?

Here have not have to Shanghai's train tickets?

B: 有。你要几点钟的?

yǒu. nǐ yào jǐ diǎn zhōng de?

Have. You want what times?

A: 三点半的

sān diǎn bàn de

Three o'clock half's

B: 要几张?

yào jǐ zhāng?

What how many?

A: 一张。到上海要坐多久?

yì zhāng. dào shàng hǎi yào zuò duō jiǔ?

One. To Shanghai have to sit how long?

B: 一般来说，三个小时

yì bān lái shuō, sān gè xiǎo shí

In general, three hours

Vocabulary

卖（mài），to sell

票（piào），ticket

到（dào），to

一般来说（yì bān lái shuō），in general / generally speaking

上（shàng），up / to get on

下（xià），down / to get off

面包车（miàn bāo chē），mini-van

迷你巴士（mí nǐ bā shì），mini-bus

卡车（kǎ chē），truck

码头（mǎ tóu），dock

长途车站（cháng tú chē zhàn），long distance bus station

铁路（tiě lù），railway

动车（dòng chē），EMU Train高铁（gāo tiě），High-Speed Train

地铁（dì tiě），underground train

Phrases

车站在哪（chē zhàn zài nǎ）?

Where is the train station / bus stop?

上车（shàng chē）

Board the train / get on the bus / get in the taxi

下车（xià chē）

Get off the train / get off the bus / get out of the taxi

到北京的火车在哪里（dào běi jīng de huǒ chē zài nǎ lǐ）?

Where is the train to Beijing?

这辆公交车不是到书店的吗（zhè liàng gōng jiāo chē bú shì dào shū diàn de ma）?

Is this bus to the bookstore?

我在等九点到上海的火车（wǒ zài děng jiǔ diǎn dào shàng hǎi de huǒ chē）

I'm waiting for the train at 9 o'clock to Shanghai

你的座位是几号（nǐ de zuò wèi shì jǐ hào）?

What is your seat number?

你能帮我照看下行李吗（nǐ néng bāng wǒ zhào kàn xià xíng li ma）?

Could you please keep an eye on my luggage?

Notes

Buying train tickets

The price of a trip often varies according to distance, and the conductor may ask you where you are going, so knowing a place name helps. If you don't like to wait in lines, you can always go to the TVM. If you are not familiar with the TVM, don't be afraid to ask for help. Chinese people will be happy to help you out.

Tip: Mistakes and learning grammar

One of the best ways to learn grammar is through experimentation. The process by which people most naturally learn grammar is called successive approximation; in other words, at first, people use simple but flawed sentences and gradually refine them by trial and error until they become more accurate and complex.

It is not only okay to make many mistakes in conversation, but virtually necessary if you are to do the kind of grammar experimentation needed for learning, so one of the best ways to learn is by plunging in and speaking at every opportunity. It is less important that you get every sentence right then that you learn from your mistakes.

Colloquial Translation of Dialogue

A: Do you have train tickets to Shanghai here?

B: Yes, which train do you want?

A: The 3:30.

B: How many tickets?

A: One. How long does it take to get to Shanghai?

B: In general, three hours.

Scenario 13: Asking for Directions

Dialogue

A needs directions to the park and asks B.

A: 请问，公园在哪里?

qǐng wèn, gōng yuán zài nǎ lǐ?

May I ask, the park is where?

B: 就在前面

jiù zài qián miàn

Just up ahead

A: 远不远?

yuǎn bù yuǎn?

Far or not?

B: 不远，很近了，走路只要十分钟

bù yuǎn, hěn jìn le, zǒu lù zhī yào shí fēn zhōng

Not far, very near, by walk only ten minutes

A: 在左边吗？

zài zuǒ biān ma?

On left side?

B: 不是，在右边

bú shì, zài yòu biān

Not is. On right side

Vocabulary

远（yuǎn），far

近（jìn），near

左边（zuǒ biān），left side

右边（yòu biān），right side

左转（zuǒ zhuǎn），turn left

右转（yòu zhuǎn），turn right

直走（zhí zǒu），go straight

米（mǐ），meter

千米（qiān mǐ），kilometer

公里（gōng lǐ），kilometer

里（lǐ），half of kilometer

前面（qián miàn），ahead

后面（hòu miàn），behind

对面（duì miàn），in front of

里面（lǐ miàn），inside

外面（wài miàn），outside

洗手间（xǐ shǒu jiān），toilet / washroom

东（dōng），east

南（nán），south

西（xī），west

北（běi），north

Phrases

书店怎么走（shū diàn zěn me zǒu）？

Where is the bookstore?

洗手间在哪里（xǐ shǒu jiān zài nǎ lǐ）？

Where is the washroom?

书店就在前面（shū diàn jiù zài qián miàn）

The bookstore is ahead

洗手间在什么地方（xǐ shǒu jiān zài shén me dì fāng）？

Can you show me the way to the toilet?

附近有饭店吗（fù jìn yǒu fàn diàn ma）？

Are there any restaurants nearby?

前面有个公园（qián miàn yǒu gè gōng yuán）

There is a park ahead

直走五百米右转（zhí zǒu wǔ bǎi mǐ yòu zhuǎn）

Go straight for five hundred meters and turn right

这是什么地方（zhè shì shén me dì fāng）？

What is this place?

我们现在在哪里（wǒ men xiàn zài zài nǎ lǐ）？

Where are we?

走这边还是那边（zǒu zhè biān hái shì nà biān）？

Shall we go this way or that way?

Notes

在(zài)

In Chinese, one preposition of place, 在(zài), covers everything—in, on, at, etc.

Strategy: Asking directions

You won't be able to understand a complicated set of directions in Chinese anytime soon, but if you can ask where something is, people can always point you in the right direction. A yes/no question like "远不远？（yuǎn bù yuǎn）" also has a good chance of prompting a response that you can understand.

Colloquial Translation of Dialogue

A: Excuse me, where's the park?

B: Just up ahead.

A: Is it far?

B: No, it's very close; only ten minutes by foot.

A: Is it on the left?

B: No, it's on the right.

Scenario 14: Asking for the Time

Dialogue

A: 请问现在几点了？

qǐng wèn xiàn zài jǐ diǎn le?

May I ask, now what time?

B: 三点五十分

sān diǎn wǔ shí fēn

Three o'clock fifty minutes

A: 你是学生吗？

nǐ shì xué shēng ma?

You are student?

B: 不是，我是英语老师。但是，我也在学习汉语

bú shì, wǒ shì yīng yǔ lǎo shī. dàn shì, wǒ yě zài xué xí hàn yǔ

No, I am English teacher. But, I also am learning Chinese

A: 你已经学了多久？

nǐ yǐ jīng xué le duō jiǔ?

You already have studied how long?

B: 就几个月

jiù jǐ gè yuè

Just a few months

A: 你进步很快

nǐ jìn bù hěn kuài.

You progress very fast

B: 哪里哪里

nǎ lǐ nǎ lǐ

Where, where

Vocabulary

现在（xiàn zài）, now

几点（jǐ diǎn）, what time

点（diǎn）, o'clock

分（fēn）, minute

但是（dàn shì）, but / however

已经（yǐ jīng）, already

学习（xué xí）, to study

多久（duō jiǔ）, how long

月（yuè）, month

进步（jìn bù）, progress / to progress

天（tiān）, day

年（nián），year

做（zuò），to do

钟（zhōng），clock

习惯（xí guàn），to be accustomed to / to get used to

今天（jīn tiān），today

昨天（zuó tiān），yesterday

明天（míng tiān），tomorrow

后天（hòu tiān），the day after tomorrow

前天（qián tiān），the day before yesterday

Days of the week:

周一/礼拜一/星期一（zhōu yī / lǐ bài yī / xīng qī yī），Monday

周二/礼拜二/星期二（zhōu èr / lǐ bài èr / xīng qī èr），Tuesday

周三/礼拜三/星期三（zhōu sān / lǐ bài sān / xīng qī sān），Wednesday

周四/礼拜四/星期四（zhōu sì / lǐ bài sì / xīng qī sì），Thursday

周五/礼拜五/星期五（zhōu wǔ / lǐ bài wǔ / xīng qī wǔ），Friday

周六/礼拜六/星期六（zhōu liù / lǐ bài liù / xīng qī liù），Saturday

周日/周末/礼拜天/星期天（zhōu rì / zhōu mò / lǐ bài tiān / xīng qī tiān），Sunday

Months:

一月（yī yuè）January

二月（èr yuè）February

三月（sān yuè）March

四月（sì yuè）April

五月（wǔ yuè）May

六月（liù yuè）June

七月（qī yuè）July

八月（bā yuè）August

九月（jiǔ yuè）September

十月（shí yuè）October

十一月（shí yī yuè）November

十二月（shí èr yuè）December

Phrases

你在中国习惯吗?（nǐ zài zhōng guó xí guàn ma）

Are you used to life in China?

现在几点了?（xiàn zài jǐ diǎn le）

What time is it now?

今天几号?（jīn tiān jǐ hào）

What day is today?

明天星期几?（míng tiān xīng qī jǐ）

What day is tomorrow?

现在四点整（xiàn zài sì diǎn zhěng）

It is four o'clock now

现在两点十五（xiàn zài liǎng diǎn shí wǔ）

It is 2:15

她正在做什么?（tā zhèng zài zuò shén me）

What is she doing right now?

她正在学习（tā zhèng zài xué xí）

She's studying

他已经来中国两年了（tā yǐ jīng lái zhōng guó liǎng nián le）

He has been in China for two years

Notice here, unlike "already" in English, "已经" can't be placed at the end of a sentence

我们在这学习一个月（wǒ men zài zhè xué xí yí gè yuè）

We will study here for a month

火车几点开（huǒ chē jǐ diǎn kāi）？

When will the train leave?

飞机什么时候起飞（fēi jī shén me shí hòu qǐ fēi）？

When will the plane depart?

明天几点到北京（míng tiān jǐ diǎn dào běi jīng）？

When will you arrive in Beijing tomorrow?

你们哪天回家（nǐ men nǎ tiān huí jiā）？

What day are you going back home?

你打算什么时候再来（nǐ dǎ suàn shén me shí hòu zài lái）？

When are you planning to come back?

你什么时候有空（nǐ shén me shí hòu yǒu kòng）？

When will you be free?

周末我没时间（zhōu mò wǒ méi shí jiān）

I'm busy on the weekend

你几点到几点上班（nǐ jǐ diǎn dào jǐ diǎn shàng bān）？

What time do you work?

我明天九点来找你（wǒ míng tiān jiǔ diǎn lái zhǎo nǐ）

I'll come to get you tomorrow at 9 o'clock

请晚上八点后打电话（qǐng wǎn shàng bā diǎn hòu dǎ diàn huà）

Please call me after 8 p.m.

你等多久了（nǐ děng duō jiǔ le）？

How long you have been waiting?

Notes

Tip: Morale in language learning

Sometimes learning Chinese can seem hopeless as there is so much to learn, and your progress seems so slow. This is less of a problem during the first few exciting days of Chinese study than later as studying becomes less fresh and new, but even early on, it can be a problem.

To keep yourself going, it helps to take things one step at a time rather than brooding over how far away the goal of total mastery is. Set a series of limited and reasonable goals for yourself, and then keep putting one foot in front of the other until you achieve them. Every time you reach a little goal, reward yourself with a pat on the back, a chocolate bar, and a satisfying look back at what you have already learned. Success in language learning has more to do with persistence in making small steps than it does with any magical talent for languages.

Colloquial Translation of Dialogue

A: Excuse me, what time is it now?

B: 3:50.

A: Are you a student?

B: No, I'm an English teacher. But I am also studying Chinese.

A: How long have you been studying?

B: Just a few months.

A: Your progress is fast.

B: Thank you.

Scenario 15: Making an Appointment

Dialogue

Foreigner A needs a haircut and hopes her Chinese acquaintance, Mr. Wang, will come along to provide assistance and moral support.

A: 王先生，你下午有没有空？

wáng xiān shēng, nǐ xià wǔ yǒu méi yǒu kòng?

Mr. Wang, you afternoon have free time?

B: 什么事？

shén me shì?

What matter?

A:
不好意思麻烦你，但是你可以陪我去剪头发吗？剪完头发以后，我请你喝咖啡

bù hǎo yì sī má fán nǐ, dàn shì nǐ kě yǐ péi wǒ qù jiǎn tóu fà ma? jiǎn wán tóu fà yǐ hòu, wǒ qǐng nǐ hē kā fēi

Embarrassed to trouble you, but you can accompany me go out cut hair? Cut hair after, I invite you to drink coffee

B: 你不用这么客气。我们几点在哪里见面？

nǐ bú yòng zhè me kè qì. wǒ men jǐ diǎn zài nǎ lǐ jiàn miàn?

You not necessary so polite. We what time at where meet?

A: 我们三点在理发店见面，好吗？

wǒ men sān diǎn zài lǐ fà diàn jiàn miàn, hǎo ma?

We 3:00 o'clock at barbershop meet, okay?

B: 好的，下午见

hǎo de, xià wǔ jiàn

Okay, afternoon see

Vocabulary

下午（xià wǔ），afternoon

请（qǐng），to treat

事（shì），business / matter

这么（zhè me），so

客气（kè qi），polite

不好意思（bù hǎo yì sī），embarrassed / excuse me

陪（péi），to accompany

见面（jiàn miàn），to meet together

剪（jiǎn），to cut

理发店（lǐ fà diàn），barbershop

头发（tóu fà），hair

以后（yǐ hòu），after

问题（wèn tí），question

早上（zǎo shàng），morning

晚上（wǎn shàng），evening

请教（qǐng jiào），to respectfully ask

以前（yǐ qián），before

Phrases

我想问你一个问题（wǒ xiǎng wèn nǐ yí gè wèn tí）

I want to ask you a question

我想请教你一个问题（wǒ xiǎng qǐng jiào nǐ yí gè wèn tí）

I want to ask you a question

Although the translations are the same, the second one is a very polite way to introduce a question to an older person or someone of higher status

我想请你吃饭（wǒ xiǎng qǐng nǐ chī fàn）

I want to treat you to a meal

下午/早上/晚上/明天/机场/门口/楼下见（xià wǔ / zǎo shàng / wǎn shàng / míng tiān / jī chǎng / mén kǒu / lóu xià jiàn）

See you in the afternoon / morning / evening / tomorrow at the airport / gate / downstairs吃饭前我们做点什么？（chī fàn qián wǒ men zuò diǎn shén me

What shall we do before we eat?

到北京后我们去爬长城吧！（dào běi jīng hòu wǒ men qù pá cháng chéng ba）

Let's visit the Great Wall after we arrive in Beijing!

我们下午三点在图书馆见面吧（wǒ men xià wǔ sān diǎn zài tú shū guǎn jiàn miàn ba）

Let's meet in the library at three o'clock in the afternoon

对不起，我有约了（duì bù qǐ, wǒ yǒu yuē le）

Sorry, I've got plans

那么就定下来了，如果来不了，请打电话给我（nà me jiù dìng xià lái le, rú guǒ lái bù liǎo, qǐng dǎ diàn huà gěi wǒ）

Then that's settled. Please call me if you can't make it

她打电话来取消约会（tā dǎ diàn huà lái qǔ xiāo yuē huì）

She phoned to cancel the appointment

我不得不把约会从周一改到周四（wǒ bù dé bù bǎ yuē huì cóng zhōu yī gǎi dào zhōu sì）

I've got to change my appointment from Monday to Thursday

他早晨在网上买了火车票（tā zǎo chén zài wǎng shàng mǎi le huǒ chē piào）

He bought a train ticket online this morning

你有预约吗？（nǐ yǒu yù yuē ma）

Do you have an appointment?

你能在这里等一下吗？（nǐ néng zài zhè lǐ děng yí xià ma）

Could you wait here for a minute?

你一点也没变（nǐ yì diǎn yě méi biàn）

You haven't changed at all

Notes

Strategy: Making Chinese friends

Often you need to take some initiative to make Chinese friends, and one good strategy is to approach Chinese people for help or with questions about working, sightseeing, and living in China. There is much, after all, that you need to learn, and your need for assistance plays to a deep-felt Chinese desire to be good hosts and help guests. Such an approach also puts you in a student role which "gives face" to whomever you ask for help. Sometimes little else grows out of such conversations, but sometimes, they serve to break the ice and start a friendship.

Colloquial Translation of Dialogue

A: Mr. Wang, do you have some free time this afternoon?

B: What's up?

A: I hate to bother you, but could you go with me to help me get a haircut? After the haircut, I'll treat you to a cup of coffee.

B: You don't need to be so polite; when should we meet and where?

A: How about meeting at 3:00 at the barber's?

B: Okay. See you this afternoon.

Scenario 16: Introducing Yourself

Dialogue

A is a curious Chinese student who has encountered foreigner B and B's two companions at a store. A strikes up a conversation.

A: 请问，你是从哪个国家来的？

qǐng wèn, nǐ shì cóng nǎ gè guó jiā lái de?

Please ask, you are from which country come?

B: 我从英国来的

wǒ cóng yīng guó lái de

I am from England come

A: 你在中国做什么？

nǐ zài zhōng guó zuò shén me?

You in China do what?

B: 我要去北京看长城

wǒ yào qù běi jīng kàn zhǎng cháng chéng

I want go to Beijing see the Great Wall

A: 他们呢？

tā men ne?

Them?

B: 他们是美国人，也要去北京

tā men shì měi guó rén, yě yào qù běi jīng

They are Americans, also want to go to Beijing

Vocabulary

从（cóng），from

哪（nǎ），which

来（lái），to come

国家（guó jiā），country

英国（yīng guó），England

中国（zhōng guó），China

美国（měi guó），America

工作（gōng zuò），work / job / to work

学生（xué shēng），student

小学（xiǎo xué），elementary school

中学（zhōng xué），middle school

大学（dà xué），university

姓（xìng），surname

名（míng），first name

老师（lǎo shī），teacher

警察（jǐng chá），police officer

工人（gōng rén），worker

司机（sī jī），driver

公务员（gōng wù yuán），government official

律师（lǜ shī），lawyer

科学家（kē xué jiā），scientist

服务员（fú wù yuán），waiter / waitress

接待员（jiē dài yuán），receptionist

厨师（chú shī），chef

Phrases

你是哪个国家的人？（nǐ shì nǎ gè guó jiā de rén）

What country are you from?

我是从英国来的（wǒ shì cóng yīng guó lái de）

I'm from England

你在哪里工作？（nǐ zài nǎ lǐ gōng zuò）

Where do you work?

我在美国工作（wǒ zài měi guó gōng zuò）

I work in America

In Chinese word order, the place must come before the predicate. In other words, while in English, you can say, "I work in America," in Chinese, you must say, "我在美国工作." It is incorrect to say, "我工作在美国."

你做什么工作（nǐ zuò shén me gōng zuò）？

What do you do?

我是老师（wǒ shì lǎo shī）

I'm a teacher

我是警察（wǒ shì jǐng chá）

I'm a police officer

请问您贵姓（qǐng wèn nín guì xìng）？

May I ask your honorable surname?

This is a polite, formal way to ask someone's name. It is appropriate especially for people whose social rank is higher or age is older than yours

你叫什么名字（nǐ jiào shén me míng zi）？

What is your name?

This is less formal and more appropriate for social equals or children

穿白衣服的那位女士是谁（chuān bái yī fú de nà wèi nǚ shì shì shuí）？

Who is the lady in white?

你能把我介绍给她吗（nǐ néng bǎ wǒ jiè shào gěi tā ma）？

Could you introduce me to her?

很高兴认识你（hěn gāo xìng rèn shí nǐ）

Nice to meet you

Notes

们 (men)

This suffix word is added to form the plural of " 我， 你， 他/她/它 ", and a few words relating to people.

Colloquial Translation of Dialogue

A: Excuse me, which country are you from?

B: I'm from England.

A: What do you do in China?

B: I want to go to Beijing to see the Great Wall.

A: And them?

B: They are Americans. They also want to go to Beijing.

Scenario 17: Talking About Family

Dialogue

A answers a knock at the door and is pleasantly surprised to find their Chinese colleague, Professor B.

A: 教授!请进来吧!

jiāo shòu! qǐng jìn lái ba!

Professor! Please enter!

B: 你好，现在忙吗?

nǐ hǎo, xiàn zài máng ma?

Hello, you now busy?

A: 不忙，不忙。进来坐

bù máng, bù máng. jìn lái zuò

Not busy, not busy. Enter come sit

B: 这张照片里的人是谁?

zhè zhāng zhào piàn lǐ de rén shì shuí?

This picture in is who?

A: 这是我父母和我妹妹

zhè shì wǒ fù mǔ hé wǒ mèi mei

There are my parents and younger sister

B: 你的爸爸做什么工作？

nǐ de bà ba zuò shén me gōng zuò?

Your father does what work?

A: 我的爸爸是司机

wǒ de bà ba shì sī jī

My father is driver

B: 你妈妈呢？

nǐ mā ma ne?

Your mother?

A: 我妈妈在医院工作

wǒ mā ma zài yī yuàn gōng zuò

My mother in hospital works

B: 你的妹妹呢？

nǐ de mèi mei ne?

Your sister?

A: 她还在上学。毕业以后她想当警察

tā hái zài shàng xué. bì yè yǐ hòu tā xiǎng dāng jǐng chá

She still is studying. Graduate after she wants to be police

Vocabulary

进（jìn），to enter

进来（jìn lái），to come in

坐（zuò），to sit / to have a seat

照片（zhào piàn），photo

父母（fù mǔ），parents

妹妹（mèi mei），younger sister

爸爸（bà ba），father

妈妈（mā ma），mother

哥哥（gē ge），older brother

姐姐（jiě jie），older sister

弟弟（dì di），younger brother

儿子（ér zi），son

女儿（nǚ ér），daughter

孩子（hái zi），child

毕业（bì yè），to graduate

家（jiā），home / family

老家（lǎo jiā），hometown

照相（zhào xiàng），to take a photo

读书/念书（dú shū / niàn shū）

Literally, this means "read books". This means " to study " in two senses:

-他还在念书（tā hái zài niàn shū）。

He's still a student.

-我们今天晚上一起读书吧（wǒ men jīn tiān wǎn shàng yì qǐ dú shū ba）。

Let's study tonight.

玩（wán），to play

This word is used for adult's recreational activities as well as children's, so it is not exactly equivalent to the English word "play".

Phrases

你家里有几口人？（nǐ jiā lǐ yǒu jǐ kǒu rén）

How many people are there in your family?

你有没有兄弟姐妹？（nǐ yǒu méi yǒu xiōng dì jiě mèi）

Do you have any brothers or sisters?

你结婚了吗？（nǐ jié hūn le ma）

Are you married?

你有孩子了吗？（nǐ yǒu hái zi le ma）

Do you have any children?

你的老家在哪里？（nǐ de lǎo jiā zài nǎ lǐ）

Where is your hometown?

我们照个相吧 wǒ men zhào gè xiàng ba）

Let's take a picture

您慢走（nín màn zǒu）

This is a fixed phrase that means "Please take care ."

有空来玩（yǒu kōng lái wán）

When you have some time, come over and visit

一路顺风（yí lù shùn fēng）

Have a safe trip

你妹妹还在学校 （nǐ mèi mei hái zài xué xiào）

Your younger sister is still in school

Notes

A few tips on politely hosting Chinese guests:

- Addressing someone by name and title when greeting your guests is considered polite and respectful in China.

- Chinese hosts will almost never turn away a guest unless strictly necessary and will apologize profusely if it is necessary to turn away a guest, even an unexpected one.

- Chinese hosts will normally offer drinks and perhaps light snacks. You may need to offer several times before a guest will take refreshments, but you should keep trying. Often it is best to simply provide refreshments rather than asking if the guest wants any—the guest will virtually always say no whether he/she wants something or not.

Strategy: Social conversation

Social conversation with new Chinese acquaintances often starts with questions about family members and what they do, and if you are in a Chinese home, there is a very good chance this conversation will be conducted over a photo album. Having a photo album is also a good strategy when you have Chinese visitors and aren't quite sure what to talk about, especially if there is no common language you both speak comfortably. You might keep a photo album of your own handy as a tool to help you conduct simple Chinese conversations with visitors or other Chinese people you meet.

Colloquial Translation of Dialogue

A: Professor! Come in!

B: How are you? Are you busy now?

A: No, no. Come in and have a seat.

B: Who are the people in this photo?

A: They are my parents, and this is my younger sister.

B: What does your father do?

A: My father is a driver.

B: Does your mother work?

A: My mother works in a hospital.

B: How about your younger sister?

A: She is still a student. But after she graduates, she wants to join the police.

Scenario 18: Personal Questions

Dialogue

Foreigner B is in the middle of her first conversation with inquisitive but helpful Chinese neighbor A.

A: 你成家了吗?

nǐ chéng jiā le ma?

You have formed family?

B: " 成家 " 是什么意思?

"chéng jiā" shì shén me yì sī?

"Formed family" is what meaning?

A: " 成家 " 就是结婚的意思

"chéng jiā" jiù shì jié hūn de yì sī

"Formed family" is to get marries meaning

B: 啊, 我没有结婚

ā, wǒ méi yǒu jié hūn

Ah, I haven't married

A: 那你多大了？

nà nǐ duō dà le?

Well, you how old?

B: 我二十七岁

wǒ èr shí qī suì

I twenty-seven years old

A: 你应该成家了。我给你介绍一个男朋友，好吗？

nǐ yīng gāi chéng jiā le. wǒ gěi nǐ jiè shào yí gè nán péng yǒu, hǎo ma?

You should form family. I for you introduce a boyfriend, okay?

B: 不用，谢谢。我觉得单身不错

bú yòng, xiè xie. wǒ jué dé dān shēn bú cuò.

Not necessary, thanks. I think single not bad

Vocabulary

成家（chéng jiā），to marry

结婚（jié hūn），to get married

老公 / 丈夫（lǎo gōng / zhàng fu），husband

老婆 / 妻子（lǎo po / qī zi），wife

爱人（ài rén），lover

岁（suì），years old

觉得（jué dé），to feel / to think that

单身（dān shēn），single

应该（yīng gāi），should

介绍（jiè shào），to introduce

男朋友（nán péng yǒu），boyfriend

女朋友（nǚ péng yǒu），girlfriend

礼貌（lǐ mào），polite

工资（gōng zī），salary

有意思（yǒu yì si），to be interesting

想（xiǎng），to miss

Phrases

你多大了?（nǐ duō dà le）?\

How old are you?

我二十二了（wǒ èr shí èr le）

I'm twenty-two years old

你结婚了吗?（nǐ jié hūn le ma）

Are you married?

我离婚了（wǒ lí hūn le）

I'm divorced

你想家吗? (nǐ xiǎng jiā ma)

Do you miss your home?

我很想家 (wǒ hěn xiǎng jiā)

I miss home very much

我一点儿也不想家 (wǒ yì diǎn ér yě bù xiǎng jiā)

I don't miss home at all

你在这里习惯吗? (nǐ zài zhè lǐ xí guàn ma)

Are you accustomed to life here?

还不太习惯 (hái bú tài xí guàn)

I'm still not very accustomed

你觉得中国怎么样? (nǐ jué dé zhōng guó zěn me yàng)

What do you think about China?

我很喜欢中国 (wǒ hěn xǐ huān zhōng guó)

I like China very much

我觉得中国很有意思 (wǒ jué dé zhōng guó hěn yǒu yì sī)

I feel China is very interesting

你一个月挣多少钱? (nǐ yí gè yuè zhèng duō shǎo qián)

How much do you make a month?

你的工资多少钱? (nǐ de gōng zī duō shǎo qián)

What is your salary?

These questions are not unusual in China. Possible answers include:

我一个月八千块钱 (wǒ yí gè yuè bā qiān kuài qián)

I make 8,000 *yuan* a month

对不起。外国人觉得这个问题让人不舒服 (duì bù qǐ. wài guó rén jué dé zhè gè wèn tí ràng rén bù shū fú)

Excuse me. Foreigners are a little uncomfortable with this question

我挣钱不多 (wǒ zhèng qián bù duō)

I don't make much

我工资不高 (wǒ gōng zī bù gāo)

My salary is not high

Notes

Many Chinese will be curious about you, and as you get into conversations, you will be asked some questions that would be considered overly personal in Western countries. Of course, it is up to you to decide how much or little to say when answering these questions, but try not to take offense to them. Such questions are generally not ill-intended, and a rude response on your part may only confuse and offend someone who has no idea why you suddenly became so testy.

Colloquial Translation of Dialogue

A: Have you formed a family?

B: What does "formed a family" mean?

A: "Formed a family" means to get married.

B: Ah, I'm not married.

A: Oh, how old are you?

B: I'm twenty-seven.

A: You should get married. Why don't I introduce you to someone?

B: That's not necessary, thanks. I think being single isn't too bad.

Scenario 19: Politely Refusing Requests

Dialogue

B: 你是美国人吗?

nǐ shì měi guó rén ma?

You are American?

A: 是的

shì de

Yes

B: 我在学英语，但是我没有机会练习。你愿意教我英语吗?

wǒ zài xué yīng yǔ, dàn shì wǒ méi yǒu jī huì liàn xí. nǐ yuàn yì jiāo wǒ yīng yǔ ma?

I am learning English, but I don't have opportunity to practice. You willing to teach me English?

A: 对不起，我在学校已经有很多学生了

duì bù qǐ, wǒ zài xué xiào yǐ jīng yǒu hěn duō xué shēng le

Sorry, I at school already have many students

B: 那我周天去找你好吗？

nà wǒ zhōu tiān qù zhǎo nǐ hǎo ma?

Then, I Sundays go look for you, okay?

A: 很抱歉，我实在太忙了

hěn bào qiàn ，wǒ shí zài tài máng le

Very sorry. I really too busy

Vocabulary

机会（jī huì），opportunity

练习（liàn xí），to practice

愿意（yuàn yì），to be willing

那么（nà me），well / in that case

找（zhǎo），to look for / to visit

实在（shí zài），really / truly

忙（máng），busy

抱歉（bào qiàn），sorry

交换（jiāo huàn），to exchange

朋友（péng yǒu），friend

Phrases

Two requests foreigners often encounter in China are:

我想练习英语（wǒ xiǎng liàn xí yīng yǔ）

I want to practice English

我们做朋友吧（wǒ men zuò péng yǒu ba）

Let's become friends

我很忙（wǒ hěn máng）

I'm very busy

我的工作很忙（wǒ de gōng zuò hěn máng）

I have a lot of work to do

我没有时间（wǒ méi yǒu shí jiān）

I don't have time

我很乐意，但我恐怕没时间（wǒ hěn lè yì, dàn wǒ kǒng pà méi shí jiān）

I'm glad to, but I'm afraid I don't have time

我们做个交易，好吗?（wǒ men zuò gè jiāo yì, hǎo ma）

Let's make a deal, okay?

This sentence is useful if you want to do an exchange, for example, English lessons for Chinese.

Notes

Strategy: Refusing requests

One problem that foreigners who want to learn Chinese often have in China is that many eager people would love to practice English with a foreigner. Thus, there is a fairly good chance that you will get more offers to practice English than you care to accept, sometimes from total strangers. When you want to refuse, the most common strategy is generally to plead that you are too busy—this excuse is not offensive and is understandable. Suitors may not give up easily, but if you politely persist, you can usually prevail.

Tip: Focusing your efforts

As you move into your work, you will probably have less time for studying Chinese, and your progress in Chinese may well slow down. This is especially a problem if you maintain a full program of study, working simultaneously on speaking, listening, reading, and writing because the more spread out your efforts are, the less progress you will feed into any particular skill area, and the greater the chance that you will become discouraged and quit.

One solution is to devote enough time to studying Chinese that you still make satisfactory progress in all areas. However, an alternative, which is often more realistic, is to narrow the range of your efforts, for example, by just working on speaking and listening for a period, or by focusing heavily on characters for a while. Having a sense of progress is vitally important in maintaining the will to keep studying, and the narrower the range of your efforts is, the more progress you will see in that one area.

Colloquial Translation of Dialogue

B: Are you an American?

A: Yes.

B: I'm studying English, but I don't have a chance to practice. Can you teach me English?

A: Sorry. I already have many students at school.

B: In that case, how about I visit you on Sundays?

A: I'm sorry. I'm really too busy.

Scenario 20: Dealing with the Delivery Company (I)

Dialogue

A is handing two unstamped letters to B, a clerk in a delivery company.

B: 要寄到哪里？

yào jì dào nǎ lǐ?

Want to send to where?

A: 到加拿大。寄到加拿大多少钱？

dào jiā ná dà. jì dào jiā ná dà duō shǎo qián?

To Canada. Send to Canada how much money?

B: 到加拿大要五十元。几封信？

dào jiā ná dà yào wǔ shí yuán. jǐ fēng xìn?

To Canada fifty *yuan*. How many letters?

A: 两封。我再买几张邮票

liǎng fēng. wǒ zài mǎi jǐ zhāng yóu piào

Two letters. I also buy several stamps

Vocabulary

寄（jì），to mail

哪里（nǎ lǐ），where

加拿大（jiā ná dà），Canada

买（mǎi），to buy

再（zài），also / again

包裹（bāo guǒ），package

邮票（yóu piào），stamp

快递公司（kuài dì gōng sī），delivery company

收件人（shōu jiàn rén），receiver

寄件人（jì jiàn rén），sender

爱尔兰（ài ěr lán），Ireland

丹麦（dān mài），Denmark

澳大利亚（ào dà lì yà），Australia

俄罗斯（é luó sī），Russia

德国（dé guó），Germany

菲律宾（fēi lǜ bīn），Philippines

韩国（hán guó），Korea

挪威（nuó wēi），Norway

瑞典（ruì diǎn），Sweden

新西兰（xīn xī lán），New Zealand

意大利（yì dà lì），Italy

法国（fǎ guó），France

芬兰（fēn lán），Finland

荷兰（hé lán），Netherland

日本（rì běn），Japan

泰国（tài guó），Thailand

Phrases

我想寄个件（wǒ xiǎng jì gè jiàn）

I want to send a package

收件地址是美国（shōu jiàn dì zhǐ shì měi guó）

The receiver's address is in America

包裹从北京到美国要多久（bāo guǒ cóng běi jīng dào měi guó yào duō jiǔ）？

How long does it take for a package to get to America from Beijing?

要想快点的话就发个特快专递（yào xiǎng kuài diǎn de huà jiù fā gè tè kuài zhuān dì）

If you want it to be quick, you can send an express mail

Notes

Tip: Practice makes perfect

By now, you may be getting tired of practicing numbers and buying. However, in language studies, there is much to be said for practicing something until you can do it rapidly and almost automatically. One of the arts of language studies is finding variations on basic forms of practice so that you can get the repetition you need without becoming so bored that your mind switches off.

Colloquial Translation of Dialogue

B: Where do you want to send this?

A: Canada. How much does it cost?

B: Fifty yuan. How many letters?

A: Two. I'll also buy several stamps.

Scenario 21: Dealing with the Delivery Company (II)

Dialogue

Foreigner A arrives at the delivery company with a package notice clutched firmly in hand. B is a postal worker.

A: 我来取包裹

wǒ lái qǔ bāo guǒ

I come get package

B: 哪里寄来的?

nǎ lǐ jì lái de?

Where sent?

A: 美国

měi guó

America

B: 有没有带证件?

yǒu méi yǒu dài zhèng jiàn?

Have not have identification?

A: 有，这是我的护照

yǒu, zhè shì wǒ de hù zhào

Have. This is my passport

Vocabulary

排队（pái duì），to stand in line

护照（hù zhào），passport

东西（dōng xī），thing

证件（zhèng jiàn），identification

身份证（shēn fèn zhèng），ID card

工作证（gōng zuò zhèng），work permit

居留证（jū liú zhèng），residence permit

签证（qiān zhèng），visa

拿（ná），to get / to take / to carry

带（Dài），to take / to bring

Phrases

在哪里排队?（zài nǎ lǐ pái duì）

Where should I line up?

我忘记了（wǒ wàng jì le）

I forgot

你有没有带护照?（nǐ yǒu méi yǒu dài hù zhào）

Did you bring your passport?

我一分钱没带（wǒ yì fēn qián méi dài）

I didn't bring any money

Notes

带 (Dài) and 拿 (ná)

While the usage of these two words often overlaps, there are some differences:

带 usually means to carry on one's person, to bring/take with one. For example:

你带了多少钱?（nǐ dài le duō shǎo qián）

How much money did you bring?

我忘记带钱了（wǒ wàng jì dài qián le）

I forgot to bring money with me

拿 usually means to get/take something, and also refers to the physical act of carrying something, for example:

我要去拿包裹（wǒ yào qù ná bāo guǒ）

I'm going to get a package

他忘记拿钱了（tā wàng jì ná qián le）

He forgot to get money (from somewhere)

Colloquial Translation of Dialogue

A: I've come to get a package.

B: Where is it from?

A: America.

B: Do you have any identification?

A: Yes, here is my passport.

Scenario 22: Not Feeling Well

Dialogue

At the guesthouse where she is staying, foreigner A is not feeling well and is explaining to staff B that she wants to see a doctor.

A: 我想看医生

wǒ xiǎng kàn yī shēng

I want to see a doctor

B: 你哪里不舒服?

nǐ nǎ lǐ bù shū fu?

You where uncomfortable?

A: 我的胃很痛

wǒ de wèi hěn tòng

My stomach very painful

B: 你有没有吃药?

nǐ yǒu méi yǒu chī yào?

You have not have eaten medicine?

A: 我没带药

wǒ méi dài yào

I don't have medicine

B: 我带你去医院

wǒ dài nǐ qù yī yuàn

I take you to hospital

Vocabulary

医生（yī shēng），doctor

门诊（mén zhěn），clinic

护士（hù shì），nurse

舒服（shū fu），comfortable

痛（tòng），to hurt / to be painful

病（bìng），illness / to be sick

感冒（gǎn mào），a cold / have a cold

拉肚子（lā dù zǐ），diarrhea / to have diarrhea

发烧（fā shāo），fever / to have a fever

便秘（biàn mì），constipated / to have a constipated

头痛（tóu tòng），headache / to have a headache

咳嗽（ké sou），cough / to have a cough

肿（zhǒng），to swell

断（duàn），to break

怎么了？（zěn me le），what's wrong?

挂号（guà hào），to register at hospital

地方（dì fāng），place

酸（suān），sore

痒（yǎng），itch / itchy

药（yào），medicine

胃（wèi），stomach

头（tóu），head

眼睛（yǎn jīng），eye

耳朵（ěr duo），ear

嘴巴（zuǐ bā），mouth

鼻子（bí zi），nose

喉咙（hóu long），throat

手（shǒu），hand

脖子（bó zi），neck

背（bèi），back

胸口（xiōng kǒu），chest

肚子（dù zi），abdomen

脚（jiǎo），foot

腿（tuǐ），leg

皮肤（pí fū），skin

牙齿（yá chǐ），tooth

舌头（shé tou），tongue

Phrases

你怎么了？（nǐ zěn me le）

What's wrong with you?

Said sympathetically, this is the appropriate inquiry to a person who looks sick or upset. In a sharper tone of voice, it can also be an accusing question about someone's mental competence

你今天感觉怎么样？（nǐ jīn tiān gǎn jué zěn me yàng）

How are you feeling today?

我觉得不太舒服（wǒ jué dé bú tài shū fu）

I don't feel very well

你现在觉得好点了吗？（nǐ xiàn zài jué dé hǎo diǎn le ma）

Do you feel better now?

好多了（hǎo duō le）

Much better

我想看病（wǒ xiǎng kàn bìng）

I want to see a doctor

我病了（wǒ bìng le）

I'm sick

我感冒了（wǒ gǎn mào le）

I have a cold

我拉肚子（wǒ lā dù zi）

I have diarrhea

他头疼的厉害（tā tóu téng de lì hài）

He's got a bad headache

我退烧了（wǒ tuì shāo le）

My fever is gone

我背疼（wǒ bèi téng）

I've got a pain in my back

就这儿疼（jiù zhè ér téng）

It hurts right here

吃两片药，好好休息一下（chī liǎng piàn yào, hǎo hǎo xiū xī yí xià）

Take two pills and have a good rest

祝你早日康复（zhù nǐ zǎo rì kāng fù）

I hope you'll be well soon

去哪里挂号？（qù nǎ lǐ guà hào）

Where do I register?

In a Chinese hospital or clinic, you need to register before seeing a doctor

Notes

Chinese Names of Common Medicines

考的松（kǎo dí sōng），Cortisone

抗真菌（kàng zhēn jūn），anti-fungal

红药水（hóng yào shuǐ），mercurochrome

肌肉止痛膏（jī ròu zhǐ tòng gāo），analgesic cream

止痛药（zhǐ tòng yào），pain relievers

泰诺林（tài nuò lín），Tylenol

必理通（bì lǐ tōng），Panadol

曲马多（qǔ mǎ duō），Tramal

百服宁（bǎi fú níng），Bufferin

阿司匹林（ā sī pǐ lín），aspirin

消炎药（xiāo yán yào）anti-inflammatory drugs

芬必得（fēn bì dé），Fenbid

布洛芬（bù luò fēn），Ibuprofen

感冒药（gǎn mào yào），cold medicines

抗组胺（kàng zǔ àn），antithistimines

抗生素（kàng shēng sù），antibiotics

红霉素（hóng méi sù），erythromycin

安必仙（ān bì xiān），ampicillin

阿莫灵（ā mò líng），amoxycillin

维生素片（wéi shēng sù piàn），vitamins

金施尔康（jīn shī ěr kāng），Gold Theragran

止泻药（zhǐ xiè yào），diarrhea Medicine

易蒙停（yì méng tíng），Imodium

抗恶心药（kàng è xīn yào），anti-nausea medicine

抗酸剂（kàng suān jì），antacids

Colloquial Translation of Dialogue

A: I want to see a doctor.

B: Where do you feel bad?

A: I have a terrible stomachache.

B: Have you taken any medicine?

A: I don't have any medicine.

B: I'll take you to the hospital.

Scenario 23: Getting Things Fixed

Dialogue

Foreigner A needs help from Chinese guesthouse staff B. A's ability to explain is limited, so the goal is just to get someone to come and look.

A: 请你来看看。卫生间有一点问题

qǐng nǐ lái kàn kan, wèi shēng jiān yǒu yì diǎn wèn tí

Please you come look look. Bathroom has a little problem

B: 什么问题?

shén me wèn tí?

What problem?

A: 马桶坏了，你看怎么处理

mǎ tǒng huài le, nǐ kàn zěn me chù lǐ

Toilet has broken, you look how to deal with

B: 我马上联系人来修

wǒ mǎ shàng lián xì rén lái xiū

I immediately contact people come fix

Vocabulary

看（kàn），to look

坏（huài），bad / to break

一点（yì diǎn），a little

帮忙（bāng máng），to help

热（rè），hot

冷（lěng），cold

快（kuài），fast

修理（xiū lǐ），to repair

空调（kōng diào），air conditioner

窗户（chuāng hu），window

电视（diàn shì），television

电灯（diàn dēng），light

电话（diàn huà），telephone

床（chuáng），bed

网络（wǎng luò），network

拖鞋（tuō xié），slippers

浴缸（yù gāng），bath tub

马桶（mǎ tǒng），toilet

Phrases

有问题（yǒu wèn tí）

Literally "问题" means problem or question, but in the phrase "有问题" it often means something wrong, for example:

他有问题（tā yǒu wèn tí）

There's something wrong with him

你还有问题？（nǐ hái yǒu wèn tí）

Do you have any questions?

看看（kàn kan）

This means to take a look. In Chinese, repeated verbs often have the sense of "a little" or "a bit". The following phrases have the same sense as "看看":

看一看（kàn yí kàn）

看一下（kàn yí xià）

房间里太热/冷了（fáng jiān lǐ tài rè /lěng le）

The room is too hot/cold

请帮我开门（qǐng bāng wǒ kāi mén）

Please open the door for me

请快一点 （qǐng kuài yì diǎn）

Please hurry a little

请打扫下房间（qǐng dǎ sǎo xià fáng jiān）

Please clean the room

能帮忙移一下冰箱吗？（néng bāng máng yí yí xià bīng xiāng ma）

Would you help me remove the refrigerator?

请帮我拿下外套（qǐng bāng wǒ ná xià wài tào）

Please get me my coat

给我冲杯咖啡，好吗？（gěi wǒ chōng bēi kā fēi, hǎo ma）

Could you make me a cup of coffee?

我不懂（wǒ bù dǒng）

I don't understand

我不知道（wǒ bù zhī dào）

I don't know

请你再说一遍（qǐng nǐ zài shuō yí biàn）

Please say that again

请你说慢一点（qǐng nǐ shuō màn yì diǎn）

Please speak a little more slowly

Notes

了 (le)

Whole dissertations have been written on this little word, but the simple idea is that it indicates that an action has been completed. For example:

我吃了 (wǒ chī le)

I've eaten

我走了 (wǒ zǒu le)

I left

空调坏了 (kōng tiáo huài le)

The air conditioner has broken

她开了窗户 (tā kāi le chuāng hu)

She opened the window

帮（bāng）and 帮忙（bāng máng）

Both mean " to help", but "帮" is followed by an object and "帮忙" is not. For example:

请你帮我（qǐng nǐ bāng wǒ）

Please help me

请你帮忙（qǐng nǐ bāng máng）

Please help

Tip: The unfamiliarity of a new language

One of the main problems Westerners face in studying Chinese is the sheer unfamiliarity of the language—it simply sounds so different from a Western language that initially it all seems a blur of sound. Do not despair though—slowly but surely your ears will get used to the sounds and contours of Chinese if you persist and give yourself time.

Colloquial Translation of Dialogue

A: Could you come and take a look? There's something wrong with the bathroom.

B: What's the problem?

A: The toilet is broken. Could you help with this?

B: I'll ask someone to fix it immediately.

Scenario 24: A Long-distance Phone Call

Dialogue

Foreigner A wants to make a long-distance phone call in a small hotel in China. B works at the front desk. C is the operator at the hotel A calls, and D is Mr. Wang.

A: 请问，长途电话怎么打？

qǐng wèn, cháng tú diàn huà zěn me dǎ?

May I ask, long-distance phone call, how to make?

B: 电话号码是什么?我帮你打

diàn huà hào mǎ shì shén me? wǒ bāng nǐ dǎ

Phone number is what? I help you call

A: 不用，我自己打

bú yòng, wǒ zì jǐ dǎ

Not necessary, I myself call

A: 金山酒店吗?

jīn shān jiǔ diàn ma?

Golden Mountain Hotel?

C: 请说大声一点，我听不见

qǐng shuō dà shēng yì diǎn, wǒ tīng bú jiàn

Please speak louder a little, I listen not hear

A: 金山酒店吗?

jīn shān jiǔ diàn ma?

Golden Mountain Hotel?

C: 是的，你找谁?

shì de, nǐ zhǎo shuí?

Is. You look for who?

A: 请转306房间

qǐng zhuǎn sān líng liù fáng jiān

Please forward 306 room

D: 喂?

wéi?

Hello?

A: 王先生在不在?

wáng xiān shēng zài bú zài?

Mr. Wang there not there?

D: 我就是

wǒ jiù shì

I am

Vocabulary

长途（cháng tú），long distance

不用（bú yòng），it's not necessary

自己（zì jǐ），self

大声（dà shēng），loud

怎么（zěn me），how

找（zhǎo），to look for

谁（shuí），who

打电话（dǎ diàn huà），make a phone call

房间（fáng jiān），room

转接（zhuǎn jiē），to forward

错（cuò），wrong

分机号（fēn jī hào），extension number

清楚（qīng chǔ），clear

国际（guó jì），international

直拨（zhí bō），direct dial

Phrases

你打错了（nǐ dǎ cuò le）

You called the wrong number

你会不会说英语？（nǐ huì bú huì shuō yīng yǔ）

Can you speak English?

This sentence is useful if a Chinese speaker answers the phone and you need to hint that you would like to speak to someone who knows English

请再说一遍（qǐng zài shuō yí biàn）

Please say that once again

我是外国人，我听不懂（wǒ shì wài guó rén, wǒ tīng bù dǒng）

I am a foreigner. I don't understand

This sentence is useful when you answer the phone and find yourself bombarded with more Chinese than you are ready to handle yet

请说大声一点（qǐng shuō dà shēng yì diǎn）

Please speak a little louder

请讲慢一点（qǐng jiǎng màn yì diǎn）

Please speak a little slower

请讲清楚一点（qǐng jiǎng qīng chǔ yì diǎn）

Please speak a little more clearly

他不在，我能替他捎个口信吗?（tā bú zài, wǒ néng tì tā shāo gè kǒu xìn ma）

He's not in, may I take a message for him?

我一定是拨错号了（wǒ yí dìng shì bō cuò hào le）

I must have dialed a wrong number

我打不通（wǒ dǎ bù tōng）

I couldn't get through

我得挂了（wǒ děi guà le）

I have to hang up

你能明天回个电话吗?（nǐ néng míng tiān huí gè diàn huà ma）

Can you call back tomorrow?

我试着给你打电话，但老占线（wǒ shì zhe gěi nǐ dǎ diàn huà, dàn lǎo zhàn xiàn）

I tried to call you, but the line was busy

Notes

Strategy: Using the phone in Chinese

Using a phone in a foreign language tends to be intimidating because the sound often isn't clear, and you can't see the expression and gestures of whomever you are talking to. However, when the phone rings, you have one great advantage—predictability. The first question the caller will ask 90 percent of the time is "Is so-and-so there?" so successfully answering the phone is largely a matter of having strategies to get the caller to slow down and let you clearly hear the name of the person they want to talk to. Likewise, making a phone call mainly involves getting to the right extension and then finding out if the person you want to talk to is there or not. Most of the time, the few basic sentences in this lesson will get you where you want to go.

Colloquial Translation of Dialogue

A: Excuse me, how do I make a long-distance phone call?

B: What is the phone number? I'll place the call for you.

A: That's not necessary. I'll call myself.

A: Is this the Golden Mountain Hotel?

C: Please speak a little louder; I can't hear you.

A: Is this the Golden Mountain Hotel?

C: Yes. Who do you wish to speak to?

A: Please forward me to Room 306.

D: Hello?

A: Is Mr. Wang there?

D: Speaking.

Epilogue: Making a Plan for Your Chinese Studies

Hopefully, you have enjoyed this book and learned something! You may use the book flexibly according to the actual situations. It has strived to make Chinese easier to learn so that readers can study the language happily, effortlessly, and efficiently.

As mentioned at the beginning of this book, there are different methods for using this book. Therefore, it is encouraged that you make plans for your long-term Chinese studies. As you go about making these plans, you need to be realistic about the fact that independent language study also poses some special problems, and a plan of study which doesn't take these problems into account has a relatively low chance of success. Here are a few of the issues you need to consider:

1- **Limits on your time and energy:** Presumably, most foreigners who can study Chinese full-time will be in formal language programs (both for academic and visa reasons), so those who take an independent study approach are often in China for work-related or travel-related reasons and generally have job, family or other obligations, which make it impossible to study Chinese full time. This means that finding time in your schedule for Chinese lessons, study, and practice may be difficult, and your other obligations which generally seem more immediately pressing, may encroach on—and even overwhelm—your Chinese study. Even if you have enough time in your schedule for a regular but limited study program, you will need to be on guard against discouragement because your progress under such circumstances may only be gradual.

2- **Absence of outside pressure:** One of the great advantages of formal language programs is that tests, grades, and the watchful eye of the teacher provide constant pressure to keep studying. Students in formal programs are often forced to keep studying, and when their will fails, there are external prods to ensure that their efforts don't decrease. On the contrary, as an independent learner, you will usually be under little or no outside pressure to keep studying Chinese. There are usually no tests to worry about, and even no tutor (if you don't find one) to pressure you. Also, foreigners who don't speak Chinese can generally get by in China using English (though the results often aren't very pretty), so pressure from the environment is much weaker than one might initially imagine. All of this means that you will probably be tempted from time to time by the knowledge that you can choose to put off studying Chinese—or even give it up completely— more or less at will. Much is therefore demanded of your will power and self-discipline, more than is the case for students in formal programs.

3- **Absence of structure:** While the goals and methods of a formal language program may not fully match the needs of a given learner, a structured program spares that learner the effort of creating a study program from scratch, and also provides the learner with a sense of direction and progress through the program. In contrast, as an independent learner, more is demanded of you because you need to design your own program. At the practical level, this means going through the effort of setting your own goals, choosing your own study materials and methods, finding a tutor (if necessary), and finding ways to evaluate and measure your progress. At the affective level, you may also be less certain about whether or not your approach to Chinese study is "right", especially if you have limited previous experience with language learning, and this sense of uncertainty may subtly corrode your confidence and resolution. This is especially likely if you adopt a very informal approach to Chinese study, doing a little of this and a little of that without much continuity or sense of a plan. Relatively unorganized study approaches often leave learners feeling that they are not learning much, either because they genuinely aren't or because the absence of structure in their approach denies them bench posts against which they can measure and see their progress, and this sets the stage for deciding that Chinese study isn't worth the effort.

As you have probably noticed, the underlying theme in the problems discussed above is not so much one of technique as it is of feelings, and this suggests one of the most basic truths of language learning: the key to success in language learning is generally sustained effort more than a special technique or language learning talents, so the most important issue is whether or not you can sustain the learning effort over a period of time. The main problem faced by most independent language learners is that it is relatively easy for them to opt out of the Chinese learning process if they become discouraged or feel they are not making enough progress to justify the effort. Designing a good study plan is thus, to a large degree, a question of how to carry out a program of study that you won't give up on. With this problem in mind, here are a few suggestions you may wish to consider as you begin setting out your Chinese study program:

1- **Be realistic about your time and energy:** The first step to successfully sustaining a program of Chinese study is realistically assessing how much time and energy you have to devote to the task, and then designing a study approach that fits within the time you have available. A common mistake that learners make, especially when just starting out with Chinese study, is making an overly optimistic assessment of their time and energy, and then setting goals that are far too high. The problem here is that when learners begin running out of steam, and especially if they fall far below the goals they set, they often get discouraged and quit, either putting off Chinese study until they have more time (a situation which often never materializes) or simply abandoning the effort altogether.

The first step to realistic planning is making a good assessment of how much time a day you can devote to studying Chinese, and also being realistic about how much energy you will have at those times of day when you are free to study. Obviously, you cannot expect to learn as much in an hour of study at a time of day when you are exhausted as you could in an hour when you are fresh and alert. Therefore, you don't need to be harsh on yourself. But remember, learners who stick with sustained study will continue to make progress, and even slow-but-steady study efforts can deliver impressive results if sustained.

2- **Setting limited goals and focusing your efforts:** As suggested above, overly ambitious goals often undermine learners' morale, so you must set reasonably limited goals that you can realistically achieve with the time and energy you have available. One implication of this idea is that it is often wise to focus on a relatively narrow set of goals, especially during the early stages of learning Chinese. For example, it might make more sense for busy people to focus their initial efforts on speaking and listening, only turning later to Chinese characters. The difficulty with trying to make a full-scale assault on Chinese, working on speaking, listening, reading, and writing simultaneously, is that dividing limited time among so many goals will probably result in slow progress toward each, and this tends to be discouraging. In contrast, a narrower focus allows you to make more visible progress in the skills of areas you focus on and encourages you to keep going.

3- **Reward:** Independent Chinese study places more demands on your self-discipline than formal Chinese classes do. As noted above, even if you work with a tutor, there will still be less outside pressure placed on you than would be the case in formal Chinese classes, and there may also be periods when you cannot find a suitable tutor—and when you therefore don't have a tutor to drive your study efforts. Thus, you need to supply the discipline for your learning process if you don't want the whole thing to dissolve into a puddle of good intentions.

When it comes to persuading yourself to study Chinese at the crack of dawn or after a long day at work, you are more likely to study properly if you are doing something you find enjoyable, rewarding, or at least useful. Thus, someone who loves to chat will probably have more motivation for sessions with a tutor, or perhaps for learning some new phrases to try out in a Chinese restaurant, while someone who is fascinated by Chinese characters may be willing to sit down and draw characters with a brush when he/she wouldn't have enough motivation to listen to audios. Know yourself, and as much as possible, design your study approach so that your interests pull you along.

4- **Structure:** Some people learn fairly well just doing whatever they feel like doing on any given day, but for most people, a casual, irregular approach to language learning is a recipe for failure. Perhaps the greatest problem with unstructured approaches to language learning is that they lack the visible indications of achievement that are present in more structured approaches, and learners who do not have the advantage of the encouragement provided by these measures of achievement are more prone to a sense that they aren't making progress.

There are a variety of ways that structure can be introduced into independent Chinese study. One of the most obvious is through the use of a textbook or other Chinese study materials—your progress through the materials provides a visible sense of satisfaction and accomplishment. Another is through setting and adhering to a regular schedule of study and practice. In this case, the amount of your time investment becomes a measure of achievement. A third, less obvious, approach involves establishing a cycle of activities that you carry out for each lesson in your book or topic that you study. For example, a cycle might consist of: Step 1 – Studying a certain lesson in your book; Step 2 – Practicing material from the lesson with a tutor; Step 3 – Trying the new material out in the community, for example, by chatting with the waitress at the nearby Chinese restaurant; and Step 4 – At the next lesson, asking your tutor about anything puzzling that occurred in your practical practice. In this approach, achievement is measured in the number of cycles you carry out. One advantage of this approach is that it not only provides structure for your program but also includes a healthy dose of live practice.

5- **Find a support group:** To a degree that might be surprising, your ability to sustain the study of Chinese will be affected by the company you keep. Unlike learners in formal Chinese programs, who have a ready-made support group of fellow learners, many of the people you live and work with—especially other Westerners—may not share your interest in learning Chinese. If this is the case, you will probably get only minimal encouragement in your efforts learning Chinese, and you may well face at least some social pressure not to devote too much time to Chinese. Keep in mind that many Westerners in China explain their failure to learn Chinese by arguing that it is simply too hard, and your progress in Chinese might make others look bad by comparison. It is thus important that you try to find at least one or two people—either other Westerners or Chinese—who will support and encourage you as you learn Chinese.

6- **Making your own plan:**

The strategy carried out by the suggestions above is that you need to take charge of your language learning by investing time in making your own plan for studying Chinese. Among the issues that you will need to consider are:

- *What are your initial study goals?* For example, do you wish initially to focus on speaking and listening skills, or do you want to work on Chinese characters right from the start?

- *What study materials will you use?* For example, if you are working with a textbook, you might consider also having your tutor (if you have one) make language audios for you to increase your amount of listening practice. If so, what kind of material would be best to put on the audios?

- *How are you going to spend your study time?* Again, assuming you are working with some kind of textbook, what is the best way for you to learn the material in any given lesson? Keep in mind that different people often have very different learning styles, so through trial and error, you need to find approaches that work well for you.

- *How do you wish to spend any time you have with a tutor if you finally hired one?*

- *How will you practice the material you learn outside language class?* You need to practice if you are to really master the material you study, so it is important to find ways to practice your Chinese in the community.

Obviously, it takes some time and effort to think about all of these things, and this list of questions may have left you longing for a teacher who would simply tell you what to do. However, by deciding these issues for yourself, you take advantage of the opportunity to tailor-make your own approach to studying Chinese, an approach that suits your goals, personality, learning style, and skill levels much better than any off-the-rack Chinese class could. Learners who take control of their Chinese learning this way generally wind up with a study program that gives them a high level of return for the effort they invest, and this provides excellent conditions for significant progress in learning Chinese.

Although you have finished this particular language journey, never stop learning because it will benefit you a lot. All in all, well done for studying and completing this book, and good luck with your further studies on the Chinese language!

Check out another book by Simple Language Learning

Printed in the USA
CPSIA information can be obtained
at www.ICGtesting.com
LVHW040721070124
768333LV00027B/368